KNITTING

FROM

FAIR ISLE

15 CONTEMPORARY DESIGNS INSPIRED BY TRADITION

KNITTING
FROM
FAIR ISLE

MATI VENTRILLON
PHOTOGRAPHY BY DYLAN THOMAS
KYLE BOOKS

An Hachette UK Company
www.hachette.co.uk

First published in the Great Britain in 2020 by
Kyle Books, an imprint of
Kyle Cathie Ltd
Carmelite House
50 Victoria Embankment
London EC4Y 0DZ
www.kylebooks.co.uk

Text copyright © Mati Ventrillon 2020
Design and layout copyright © Kyle Cathie Ltd 2020
Photography copyright © Dylan Thomas 2020
Image on page 8 by Daan Craanen

Editorial Director: Judith Hannam
Publisher: Joanna Copestick
Editor: Jenny Dye
Design: Planning Unit
Photography: Dylan Thomas
Pattern writer: Rosee Woodland
Technical editor: Amelia Hodson
Models: David Bernardi and Claudia Todd
Production: Caroline Alberti

ISBN 978-0-85783-748-6

A CIP catalogue record for this book is available from
the British Library.

Printed and bound in China

10 9 8 7 6 5 4 3 2

All the garments in this book have been
created following the traditional way of
knitting in Fair Isle, with full repeats of
the 24-stitch motifs, both horizontal and
vertical; therefore, differing tensions have
been used for each garment size. The
adjustment of tension will result in
slight variations of length between
sizes that won't necessarily respond to an
increase per size. If necessary, the length
of body or sleeve can be adapted by using
a provisional cast on to allow for the ribs
to be knitted at the end in order to adjust
the length without modifying the motifs.

You may need to experiment with needle
sizes to achieve the required tension for
your size. If you've achieved the correct
stitch tension but your round/row tension
is wrong, try changing needle size by the
smallest increment available, as this will often
be enough to alter your round/row tension
without compromising your stitch tension.

If you find you can only achieve stitch tension
but not round/row tension, remember that
you can still block out a small difference
in round/row tension. Always block your
swatch in the same way that you will block
the finished garment.

The yarn quantities given are approximates,
with the MC being the most accurate; this
responds to the variation in tension through
the project and the nature of Fair Isle knitting,
as the length of floats in stranded work varies
from knitter to knitter.

CONTENTS

Opening endpaper: South Harbour
Page 2: Sheep Rock, North Haven and Buness
This page: View from Meoness

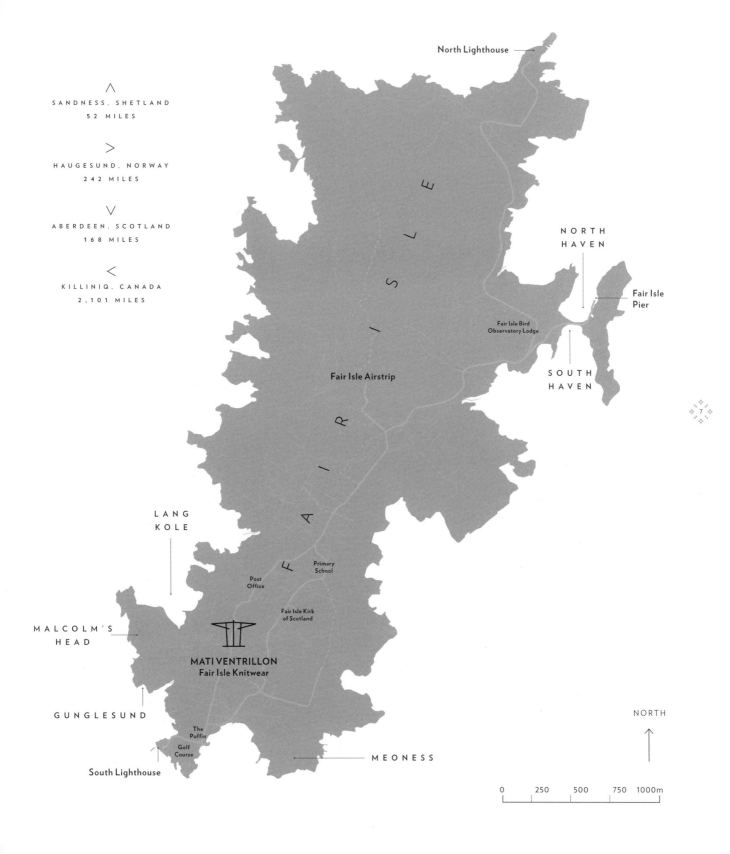

SANDNESS, SHETLAND
52 MILES

HAUGESUND, NORWAY
242 MILES

ABERDEEN, SCOTLAND
168 MILES

KILLINIQ, CANADA
2,101 MILES

North Lighthouse

NORTH
HAVEN

Fair Isle
Pier

Fair Isle Bird
Observatory Lodge

SOUTH
HAVEN

Fair Isle Airstrip

F A I R   I S L E

LANG
KOLE

Primary
School

Post
Office

Fair Isle Kirk
of Scotland

MALCOLM'S
HEAD

MATI VENTRILLON
Fair Isle Knitwear

GUNGLESUND

The
Puffin

Golf
Course

South Lighthouse

MEONESS

NORTH

0   250   500   750   1000m

Mati Ventrillon

INTRODUCTION

In 2007, I moved from London, where I was working as an architect, to Fair Isle, one of the islands that make up the Shetland Isles. It was a journey into the unknown, from one of the world's greatest cities to an agricultural community on the most remote inhabited island in the UK. Despite having no experience in either crofting or knitting, but determined to put my creative skills to work, I joined the Fair Isle Crafts Co-operative and spent four years learning about the complex traditional motifs from the very best in the business. I became intrigued by the stories of the women who spent their lives knitting masterpieces despite harsh living conditions and inclement weather. In 2011 the co-operative dissolved, but by this point I had so much love for the knits that I decided to launch my own business in an attempt to fulfil my dream of a 'Made in Fair Isle' label.

My first commission, in 2012, was a fisherman's jumper for Ben Fogle, the design of which was based on the garments worn by the crew of the Bruce Antarctic Expedition of 1904; it was my first attempt at shaping and colour work, not a simple task. That same year I was invited to take part in the Great Campaign, a showcase of British design, for which I designed the 'Oxford' jumper that later featured in Chanel's 2015 Métier d'Art pre-autumn collection. A year later, I designed a series of tea cosies for Fortnum & Mason's Mad for Tea campaign, inspired by the company's colours and their tea rooms. I also took part in two exhibitions in Somerset House in London as part of Crafted UK. It was the time when things started to happen.

Every Fair Isle knitter throughout history has imprinted his or her own identity in every piece created. My designs are inspired by traditional Fair Isle motifs from the 19th and early 20th centuries, as for me these are what make Fair Isle knitting unique. As a Fair Isle crofter, albeit in the 21st century, I continue in my own way hundreds of years of tradition. It took me several years and many mistakes to find my own identity, but I hope I can take you through that journey of pattern, shape, colour and self-discovery so that you, too, can find your very own Fair Isle style.

TRADITIONAL TOOLS AND MATERIALS

WOOL

Shetland's native sheep date back 5,000 years; they belong to the Northern European short-tailed breeds, which seem to have been spread by Norse Vikings to several countries stretching from Russia to Iceland. Shetland wool is characterised by its unique insulating properties, strength, springiness and softness. It exhibits upper hairs of several inches long and very fine lower hairs. The springiness is created by the distinct Shetland crimp. The wool shows an amazing variety of colours and patterns; there are 57 names in Norn (an extinct North Germanic language that was spoken in Orkney and Shetland), specific to colours and patterns in sheep. There are 11 main whole colours and 30 recognised markings in Shetland alone. Shetland sheep are an intrinsic part of island life.

This page top: South Green towards Gunglesund
This page below: Wool and hand carders
Opposite: Carding wool

WIRES

In Fair Isle and Shetland, the hand-knitting industry continues to be practised as it has been since the 17th century. The knitting needles are called wires and resemble early knitting needles from medieval times, where knitters used homemade needles with pointed ends made out of materials such as wood, bone, copper wire, iron, ivory or briar. Today the needles are mostly made from aluminium or iron but remain thin at UK 16 (US 00). The metric equivalent is less than 1.75mm.

Below: Knitting needles

KNITTING BELT

In Shetland the knitting belt is called a 'maakin belt' and consists of a perforated leather pouch stuffed with horse hair to make it padded. The knitting belt is used with wires (double-pointed knitting needles) and is worn at the right side, about waist level. The right needle is pushed into one of the holes in the belt pad, keeping the needle anchored as the stitches are worked, making the job easier and faster.

Shetland knitters wore their belts at all times and were able to knit while carrying out daily chores and farming activities; when friends and family gathered around the fireplace, the belt would still be firmly in place because there was still knitting to be done. The fact that knitting was never industrialised allowed women to have control of all aspects of production and to develop a cottage industry that has supplied the world with Shetland knits to supplement the family's income.

Above: Knitting belt
and needles

WOOLLIE HORSE

Woollie Horse is the brand name of the jumper board manufactured by Tulloch of Shetland up until the 1960s. A firm called Paparwark has started producing them in the same shape and quality. Made out of wood, with gold print and brass pins, the Woollie Horse is not just a tool but a masterpiece of craftsmanship. Jumper boards have been used in Shetland for many years to dress (block) garments and were mainly home made out of wood. Although the designs differ slightly, they share common features: boards have 'feet', either fixed or swivelling, which allow the board to be free standing, and a narrow piece for the shoulders and tops of sleeves, from cuff to cuff. This can either be one long piece or two pieces that are joined when needed, which makes it easier to store. The jumper board is a common feature in Shetlanders' homes.

MOTIFS

The motifs selected for the design of the garments are traditional Fair Isle motifs used by the island's knitters since or before the 19th century. They represent the island's tradition and give our knitwear its identity. I selected specifically the Muckle Flooers and the Fivey Flooers, as they are traditionally called in the island, as the main motifs for the designs. The Muckle Flooers are 17-row motifs and the Fivey Flooers are 11-row motifs. For the traditional Kep design (see page 66) I used the traditional motifs arrangement, combining Grunds or 5-row motifs with the Muckle Flooers; and in the design of the section 'Inspired by Tradition' I used an arrangement combining Muckle Flooers, Flooers and Grunds.

A Woollie Horse in Mati's studio

INSPIRED BY TRADITION

Learning about Fair Isle knitting meant learning about both colour combination and motif arrangement. As I struggled to create designs that were harmonious or looked 'Fair Isle', I turned to history and to museum pieces in an attempt to decipher the 'secret'. While photocopying a text with a couple of samples of knitted caps in black and white from c.1850 something extraordinary happened: I realised that what made Fair Isle patterns so recognisable were the motifs, the Muckle Flooers (large motifs) that appear throughout the 19th century.

My first two-colour experiment was inspired by one of the knitted caps and from there followed a two-tone garment and a scarf with the traditional colours. In this group of projects I use the motif arrangements from that original cap to explore the scale on different garments, and the use of colour, while preserving Fair Isle's identity.

Gunglesund

MOCK FINGERLESS
MITTS

Our hands are our tools for creation, the connection between our creative mind and the tangible world. This quick-to-knit project will keep your fingers free and your hands warm. Knitting fingers can be quite tricky and time consuming, so these fingerless mitts are ideal for beginners.

SIZE	S / M
To fit hand circumference measured around knuckles	15–22cm 6–8½in
Finished circumference	17.75cm 7in
Finished height	27.5cm 10¾in

YARN

Jamieson's of Shetland, Shetland Spindrift
4ply weight, 100% Shetland wool, 105m (115yd) per 25g ball

Grey colourway
- ● **2 ×** 123 Oxford **MC**
- ○ **1 ×** 122 Granite

Traditional colourway
- ● **2 ×** 587 Madder **MC**
- ● **1 ×** 726 Prussian
- ● **1 ×** 289 Gold
- ○ **1 ×** 104 Natural White

Admiral colourway
- ● **2 ×** 727 Admiral Navy **MC**
- ● **1 ×** 168 Clyde Blue
- ● **1 ×** 134 Blue Danube
- ○ **1 ×** 104 Natural White
- ● **1 ×** 578 Rust
- ● **1 ×** 478 Amber

Above: Mitts knitted by Sara Levene
Opposite: Bird watching at Gunglesund
Mitts knitted by Sara Levene

MOCK FINGERLESS MITTS

TENSION

27 stitches and 30 rounds to 10cm (4in), measured over blocked, stranded colourwork, using 3.25mm (US 3, UK 10) needles.

If necessary, change your needle size to achieve the stated tension.

NEEDLES & NOTIONS

1 set 3.25mm (US 3, UK 10) double-pointed needles or long circular needle for magic loop method

Tapestry needle

1 stitch marker

NOTES

When working colourwork sections, strand colour not in use evenly across the back (wrong side) of your work.

All chart rounds should be read from right to left, apart from Rows 20–39, which are worked back and forth in rows, starting with a RS (knit) row.

These mock fingerless mitts are worked finger-end down, with the ribbed edging later sewn together at regular intervals to create the finger openings. The slightly unusual construction method is designed to give a stylish effect with minimal effort.

INSTRUCTIONS

With MC, make a slip knot and place on needle as the first st, leaving a long tail for casting on. Cast on 1 st using the long-tail cast-on method, then cast on 2 sts using the twisted German cast-on method. *Cast on 2 sts using the long-tail cast-on method, cast on 2 sts using the twisted German cast-on method; repeat from * until there are 48 sts on the needle.

Join to work in the round, being careful not to twist. Place marker for beginning of round.

Mock fingerless mitts can be worked entirely from chart, repeating the 48-stitch pattern once per round.

If this is your preferred method, read the section on page 22 on Upper edging before working Rounds 81–82. Follow chart until you have completed Round 83, then cast off purlwise.

Alternatively, follow written pattern overleaf and refer to chart for colourwork section only.

Pattern continues overleaf

Grey colourway

48 47 46 45 44 43 42 41 40 39 38 37 36 35 34 33 32 31 30 29 28 27 26 25 24 23 22 21 20 19 18 17 16 15 14 13 12 11 10 9 8 7 6 5 4 3 2 1

☐ Knit
• Purl
◣ SSK
◡ Cast on
◇ Kwss
☐ Centre stitch
☐ Work in rows
▧ 123 Oxford
☐ 122 Granite

21

Lower edging

Rib Round: *K2, p2; rep from * to end of round.

Repeat Rib Round another 8 times.

Main section

Rounds 10–23: Knit, following chart.

Row 24 (RS): Knit, following chart, to last 2 sts, ssk using colour shown on chart. Turn. 47 sts.

Rows 25–35: Beginning with a WS (purl) row, continue working back and forth in rows, stranding colour not in use across WS of work.

Round 36: Knit to end, cast on 1 st over gap using backward loop method and pulling tightly to avoid making a loose stitch. Do not turn. 48 sts.

Rounds 37–80: Knit, following chart.

Upper edging

This edging is worked by using two separate strands of the same colour, alternating them across each round. In this way, you create a single-colour form of stranded colourwork, which will prevent the top edge of the gloves from rolling over, while remaining at the same tension as the colourwork section you will work next.

For the second strand, pull from the centre of the ball.

If you are following the chart, you will see a symbol indicating when to use the second strand, given here as kwss.

Round 81: *Kwss, k1; rep from * to end of round.

Round 82: *K1, kwss; rep from * to end of round.

Cut second strand of MC.

Round 83: Knit to end.

Cast off purlwise.

Thumb

Using MC, pick up and knit 24 sts around thumb opening (the white space on the far left of rows 24–35 on the charts).

Rib Round: *K2, p2; rep from * to end of round.

Repeat Rib Round another 9 times.

Cast off in rib.

Finishing

Turn your mitt the right way up, and from the inner top edge of the thumb opening, count 6 sts across the colourwork towards the opposite edge. Use a needle threaded with MC to sew the two sides of the mitt together vertically along the rib section only, using back stitch, to create a finger opening. Repeat this process twice more to create 4 finger openings along the ribbed top edge of the mitt.

Weave in ends and block to measurements given at the beginning of the pattern.

Repeat pattern for second mitt.

Traditional colourway

- ☐ Knit
- ⦁ Purl
- ◣ SSK
- ◡ Cast on
- ◇ Kwss
- ☐ Centre stitch
- ☐ Work in rows
- ■ 587 Madder
- ■ 726 Prussian
- ☐ 289 Gold
- ☐ 104 Natural White

23

Admiral
colourway

Knit

• Purl

╲ SSK

⏝ Cast on

◇ Kwss

Centre stitch

Work in rows

■ 727 Admiral Navy

■ 168 Clyde Blue

■ 134 Blue Danube

□ 104 Natural White

■ 578 Rust

■ 478 Amber

24

Opposite: Lang Kole

LONG HAT

This is my favourite style of hat – a simplified version of the traditional kep, lighter and slightly shorter, yet reminiscent of the fishermen's attire of the 17th and 18th centuries.

SIZE	S	M	L
To fit head circumference (approx)	47cm 18½in	55cm 21¾ in	64cm 25¼in
Actual hat circumference at brim	44.5cm 17½in	53 cm 21in	62cm 24½in
Hat length (Long hat)		30cm 11¾in	

YARN

Jamieson's of Shetland, Shetland Spindrift
4ply weight, 100% Shetland wool, 105m (115yd) per 25g ball

Grey colourway
- 2 × 123 Oxford **MC**
- 1 × 122 Granite

Traditional colourway
- 1 × 587 Madder **MC**
- 1 × 726 Prussian
- 1 × 289 Gold
- 1 × 104 Natural White

Admiral colourway
- 1 × 727 Admiral Navy **MC**
- 1 × 168 Clyde Blue
- 1 × 134 Blue Danube
- 1 × 104 Natural White
- 1 × 578 Rust
- 1 × 478 Amber

Above: Hat knitted by Julia Ryder
Opposite: Climbing at Gunglesund
Hat knitted by Connie Boster

Opposite: South lighthouse
from Gunglesund

TENSION

27 stitches and 30 rounds to 10cm (4in), measured
over blocked stranded colourwork, using 3.25mm (US 3,
UK 10) needles.

If necessary, change your needle size to achieve the
stated tension.

NEEDLES & NOTIONS

1 set 2.75mm (US 2, UK 12) double-pointed needles or long
circular needle for magic loop method

1 set 3.25mm (US 3, UK 10) double-pointed needles or long
circular needle for magic loop method

1 stitch marker plus 4 (5: 6) stitch markers, in a contrasting
colour (optional)

Tapestry needle

NOTES

When working colourwork sections, strand colour not in use
loosely across the back (wrong side) of your work.

All chart rows should be read from right to left.

INSTRUCTIONS

With MC, make a slip knot and place on needle as the first
st, leaving a long tail for casting on. Cast on 1 st using the
long-tail cast-on method, then cast on 2 sts using the twisted
German cast-on method. *Cast on 2 sts using the long-tail
cast-on method, cast on 2 sts using the twisted German
cast-on method; repeat from * until there are 120 (144: 168)
sts on the needle. Join to work in the round, being careful
not to twist. Place marker for beginning of round.

Hat can be worked entirely from chart, repeating the
24-stitch pattern 5 (6: 7) times per round. If this is your
preferred method, follow chart, changing to larger needles
when rib is complete, and then follow Round 91 as written
overleaf – this round is not shown on the chart.

Alternatively, follow written pattern below and refer to
chart for colourwork section only.

Brim

Rib Round: * K2, p2; rep from * to end of round.

Work Rib Round another 4 times.

Round 6: Knit to end of round.

Main section

Work colourwork section, following Rows 7–76 of chart,
repeating the 24-stitch pattern 5 (6: 7) times per round,
and placing contrasting markers every 24 sts to denote
repeats, if desired, on first of these rounds.

Colourwork section is now complete.

Round 77: With MC only, knit to end of round, removing
any pattern repeat markers as you come to them.

Crown decreases

Round 78: *K6, k2tog; rep from * to end. 15 (18: 21) sts dec'd.
105 (126: 147) sts rem.

Round 79: Knit to end of round.

Round 80: *K5, k2tog; rep from * to end. 15 (18: 21) sts dec'd.
90 (108: 126) sts rem.

Round 81: Knit to end of round.

Round 82: *K4, k2tog; rep from * to end. 15 (18: 21) sts dec'd.
75 (90: 105) sts rem.

Round 83: Knit to end of round.

Round 84: *K3, k2tog; rep from * to end. 15 (18: 21) sts dec'd.
60 (72: 84) sts rem.

Round 85: Knit to end of round.

Round 86: *K2, k2tog; rep from * to end. 15 (18: 21) sts dec'd.
45 (54: 63) sts rem.

Pattern continues overleaf

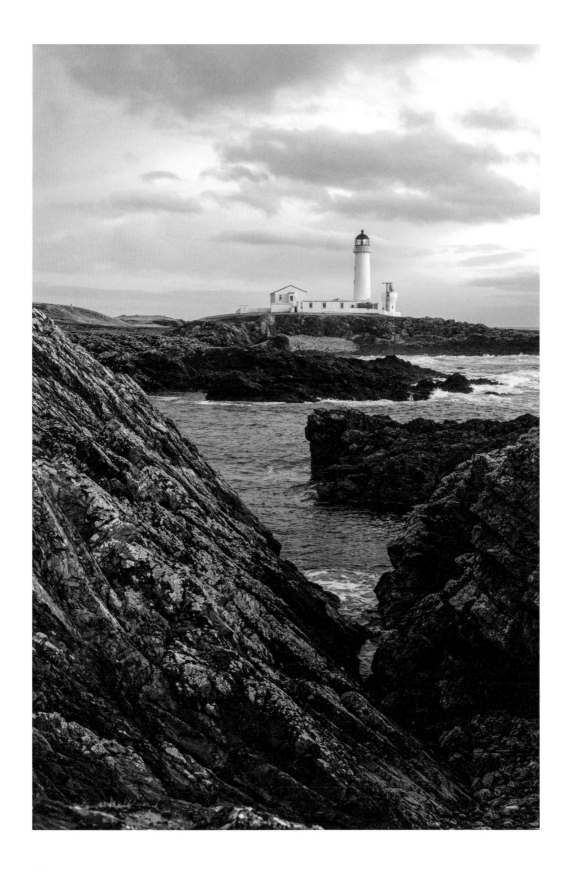

Round 87: Knit to end of round.

Round 88: *K1, k2tog; rep from * to end. 15 (18: 21) sts dec'd. 30 (36: 42) sts rem.

Round 89: Knit to end of round.

Round 90: *K2tog; rep from * to end. 15 (18: 21) sts dec'd. 15 (18: 21) sts rem.

Round 91 (not shown on chart): K1 (0: 1), *k2tog; rep from * to end. 7 (9: 10) sts dec'd. 8 (9: 11) sts rem.

Finishing

Break yarn and thread through rem sts. Pull firmly to fasten.

Weave in ends and block to measurements given at the beginning of the pattern.

Tassel

Wind 2, 3 or 4 strands of contrasting yarn lengthways around an 11cm (4¹/₄in) piece of thick card or a slim book.

If using 2 strands, wrap card 40 times.

If using 3 strands, wrap card 25 times.

If using 4 strands, wrap card 20 times.

Carefully cut the strands at one end, and at the other end use a strand of yarn to secure the tassel. Make a cord by twisting 2 strands of yarn and then use this to tie the secured centre with a knot. Wrap another strand of yarn around the tassel about 4cm (1¹/₂in) from the centre, creating a round-top ball. Attach the tassel to the crown of the hat using the two cord ends, and weave in the ends on the inside around the closed stitches.

Grey colourway

Knit

Purl

K2tog

123 Oxford

122 Granite

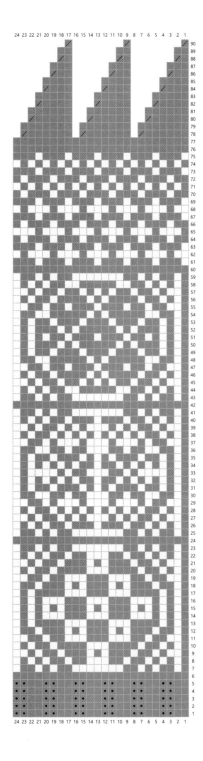

Traditional colourway

24 23 22 21 20 19 18 17 16 15 14 13 12 11 10 9 8 7 6 5 4 3 2 1

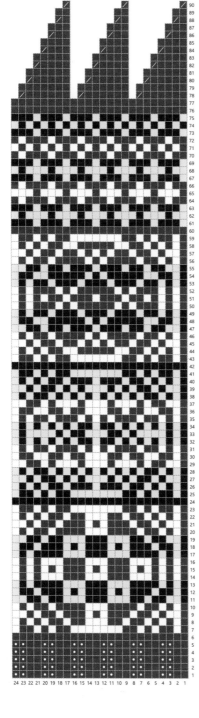

Knit

• Purl

╱ K2tog

■ 587 Madder

■ 726 Prussain Blue

▨ 289 Gold

□ 104 Natural White

Admiral colourway

24 23 22 21 20 19 18 17 16 15 14 13 12 11 10 9 8 7 6 5 4 3 2 1

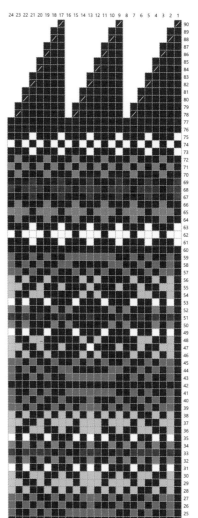

Knit

╱ Purl

• K2tog

■ 727 Admiral Navy

▨ 168 Clyde Blue

▨ 134 Blue Danube

□ 104 Natural White

■ 578 Rust

▨ 478 Amber

31

LONG SCARF

This piece is inspired by mid-19th-century men's scarves. It is slightly longer than the original versions and includes motifs that were used on Fair Isle caps during the 1850s.

SIZE	ONE SIZE
Finished width	36cm 14in
Finished length	206cm 81in

YARN

Jamieson's of Shetland,
Shetland Spindrift 4ply weight,
100% Shetland wool,
105m (115yd) per 25g ball

Grey colourway

● **6** × 123 Oxford **MC**

○ **6** × 104 Natural White

Traditional colourway

● **6** × 587 Madder **MC**

● **3** × 726 Prussian

● **3** × 289 Gold

○ **5** × 104 Natural White

Admiral colourway

● **9** × 727 Admiral Navy **MC**

● **4** × 168 Clyde Blue

● **4** × 134 Blue Danube

○ **3** × 104 Natural White

● **1** × 578 Rust

● **1** × 478 Amber

This page: Scarf knitted by Anette von Block
Opposite: Rabbit hunting at Gunglesund
Scarf knitted by Nicky Angeli

TENSION

27 stitches and 30 rows to 10cm (4in), measured over blocked stranded colourwork, using 3.25mm (US 3, UK 10) needles.

If necessary, change your needle size to achieve the stated tension.

NEEDLES & NOTIONS

1 pair 3.25mm (US 3, UK 10) straight needles

Spare 3.25mm (US 3, UK 10) straight needle

Tapestry needle

NOTES

When working colourwork sections, strand colour not in use evenly across the back (wrong side) of your work.

Read RS rows from right to left and WS rows from left to right.

	Knit
•	Purl
	Pattern repeat
	Work 5 times in total
	Work 4 times in total
	Work 2 times in total
	Work 9 times in total
	Work 13 times in total
	123 Oxford
	104 Natural White

	Knit
•	Purl
	Pattern repeat
	Work 5 times in total
	Work 4 times in total
	Work 2 times in total
	Work 9 times in total
	Work 13 times in total
	587 Madder
	726 Prussian
	289 Gold
	104 Natural White

Grey colourway

Traditional colourway

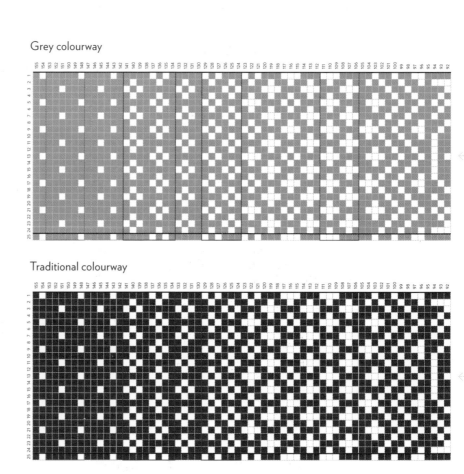

INSTRUCTIONS

First piece

With MC, cast on 97 sts.

You will work across chart, on RS rows working sts 1–24 four times, then working st 25 once and on WS rows working st 25 once, then working sts 24–1 four times.

Traditional and Grey colourways only

Follow chart to end of Row 105.

Work Rows 106–111 five times in total.
Work Rows 112–123 once.
Work Rows 124–129 four times in total
Work Rows 130–133 once.
Work Rows 134–141 twice in total.
Work Row 142 once.
Work Rows 143–146 nine times in total.
Work Row 147 once.**
Work Rows 148–153 thirteen times in total.
Work Rows 154–155 once.

Pattern continues overleaf

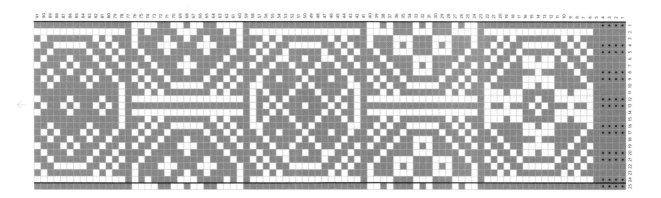

LONG SCARF

Admiral colourway only

Follow chart to end of Row 192.

Work Rows 193–196 seven times in total.
Work Rows 197–205 once.
Work Rows 206–211 twice in total.
Work Rows 212–218 once.
Work Rows 219–224 twice in total.
Work Rows 225–229 once.
Work Rows 230–235 twice in total.
Work Rows 236–242 once.
Work Rows 243–248 twice in total.**
Work Rows 249–261 once.

All colourways

Leave sts on scrap yarn or spare needles.

Second piece

Work as First Piece to **.

Traditional and Grey colourways only.

Work Rows 148–153 twelve times in total.
Work Rows 148–151 once. End here.

Admiral colourway only

Work Rows 249–257 once. End here.

All colourways

Leave sts on needles.

Finishing

With RS facing and using MC, graft the two sets of sts together using Kitchener stitch.

Weave in ends and block to measurements given at the beginning of the pattern.

Above: Fair Isle chapel at Taft Croft

Admiral
colourway

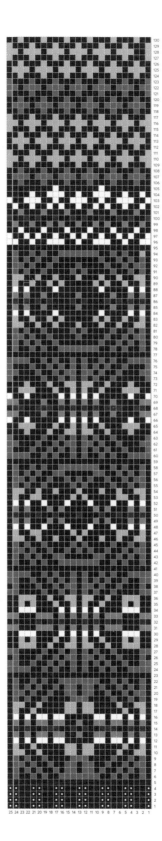

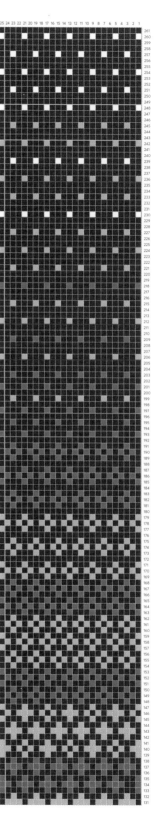

37

SLEEVELESS ROUND-NECK VEST

Adapting the traditional Fair Isle cap motifs for this vest was an interesting process, as the original vests tend to show the motifs on the upper section. The result is a light and modern-looking garment that uses 1850s Fair Isle motifs.

YARN

Jamieson's of Shetland, Shetland Spindrift 4ply weight, 100% Shetland wool, 105m (115yd) per 25g ball

Grey colourway

- 103 Oxford **MC**
- 122 Granite

Traditional colourway

- 587 Madder **MC**
- 726 Prussian
- 289 Gold
- 104 Natural White

Ombre colourway

- 727 Admiral Navy **MC**
- 168 Clyde Blue
- 134 Blue Danube
- 104 Natural White
- 578 Rust
- 478 Amber

For number of balls of yarn required for each size, refer to colourway charts.

SIZE	XS	S	M	L	XL
To fit chest circumference (approx)	81–86cm 32–34in	89–94cm 35–37in	99–104cm 39–41in	112–117cm 44–46in	122–127cm 48–50in
Actual chest circumference	89cm 35in	96cm 37¾in	107cm 42in	120cm 47¼in	128cm 50½in
Length to side shoulder, when worn	54.5cm 21½in	54cm 21¼in	59cm 23¼in	62cm 24¼in	65cm 25½in
Armhole depth (less 2.5cm / 1in edging), when worn	21.5cm 8½in	22.5cm 9in	24cm 9½in	25cm 10in	27cm 10¾in
Finished back neck width (Women's version)	15cm 5¾in	17cm 6¾in	18.5cm 7¼in	20cm 8in	21cm 8¼in
Finished back neck width (Men's version)	11cm 4¼in	11.5cm 4½in	11cm 4¼in	12cm 4¾in	12.5cm 5in
Finished front neck depth (women's version)	8cm 3in	8.5cm 3¼in	9cm 3½in	9cm 3½in	9.5cm 3¾in
Finished front neck depth (Men's version)	5cm 2in	5.5cm 2¼in	5cm 2in	5.5cm 2¼in	6cm 2½in

Above: Vest knitted by Samsara Chapman
Opposite: Sheep herding at Lower Leogh
Vest knitted by Val Smith

TENSION

All the garments in this book have been created using different tensions depending on the size being knitted. This allows us to offer a variety of sizes without having to use partial repeats of the 24-stitch patterns.

You may need to experiment with needle sizes to achieve the required tension for your size. If you've achieved the correct stitch tension but your round/row tension is wrong, try changing needle size by the smallest increment available, as this will often be enough to alter your round/row tension without compromising your stitch tension.

If you find you can only achieve stitch tension but not round/row tension, remember that you can still block out a small difference in round/row tension. Always block your swatch in the same way that you will block the finished garment. See page 141 for blocking instructions.

Sizes XS and M only

27 stitches and 30 rounds/rows to 10cm (4in), measured over blocked stranded colourwork, using 3.25mm (US 3, UK 10) needles.

If necessary, change your needle size to achieve the stated tension.

Sizes S and XL only

30 stitches and 34 rounds/rows to 10cm (4in), measured over blocked stranded colourwork, using 2.75mm (US 2, UK 12) needles.

If necessary, change your needle size to achieve the stated tension.

Size L only

28 stitches and 32 rounds/rows to 10cm (4in), measured over blocked stranded colourwork, using 3mm (US 2/3, UK 11) needles.

If necessary, change your needle size to achieve the stated tension.

NEEDLES & NOTIONS

Circular needle two sizes below the size for your required tension, 80cm (32in) long

Circular needle for the required tension, 80cm (32in) long

1 set double-pointed needles for the required tension

1 set double-pointed needles or shorter circular needle two sizes below the size for the required tension for armhole and neck edgings

1 stitch marker plus 9 (11: 11: 13: 15) stitch markers, in a contrasting colour (optional)

Tapestry needle

Small crochet hook

Needle and polyester or wool thread

Small sharp scissors

NOTES

This vest is 12 rows longer at the front top edge than at the back, to give a tailored finish to the shoulder, with a seam that sits 6 rows behind, rather than on top of, the shoulder.

When working colourwork sections, strand colour not in use evenly across the back (wrong side) of your work.

All chart rows should be read from right to left when working in the round.

When working flat in rows, read RS rows from right to left and WS rows from left to right.

Armholes are made by casting off body stitches and then casting on for steeks (see page 141), which are cut open later and stitched down.

INSTRUCTIONS

With MC and smaller circular needles, make a slip knot and place on needle as the first st, leaving a long tail for casting on. Cast on 1 st using the long-tail cast-on method, then cast on 2 sts using the twisted German cast-on method. * Cast on 2 sts using the long-tail cast-on method, cast on 2 sts using the twisted German cast-on method; repeat from * until there are 240 (288: 288: 336: 384) sts on the needle.

Join to work in the round, being careful not to twist. Place marker for beginning of round.

Follow written pattern below and refer to chart for colourwork placement only.

Hem

Rib Round: *K2, p2; rep from * to end of round.

Repeat Rib Round another 14 (16: 14: 16: 16) times.

Body

Change to larger circular needles.

Work colourwork section, repeating the 24-stitch pattern 10 (12: 12: 14: 16) times each for round, and placing markers after each repeat to denote repeats, if desired, on first of these rounds.

Continue in colourwork pattern until you have completed Row 76 (90: 82: 92: 104) of chart, ending last round 4 (5: 6: 7: 8) sts before end of round.

Shape armholes and set steeks

Next Round: Cast off 8 (10: 12: 14: 16) sts, pattern until you have 112 (134: 132: 154: 176) sts on your needles, cast off the next 8 (10: 12: 14: 16) sts, pattern 112 (134: 132: 154: 176) sts to end of round, noting that the first of these sts will already be on your right needle after casting off. DO NOT BREAK YARN.

You will now cast on for steeks across both armholes.

Next Round: Using the backwards loop method and MC, cast on 7 sts across left underarm cast off, pattern across 112 (134: 132: 154: 176) sts for Front, cast on 7 sts across right underarm cast off, pattern across 112 (134: 132: 154: 176) sts for Back. 238 (282: 278: 322: 366) sts total; 112 (134: 132: 154: 176) sts each for Front and Back and 7 sts per steek.

When working steek stitches, use two colours, alternating every other stitch to create a chequerboard or stripe effect.

Steeks should always be worked as follows: P1, k5, p1.

Purling at the edges of the steek allows you to fold back the edge easily later.

Shape armholes

Keeping steek and colourwork pattern correct, decrease 1 st at each armhole edge on next 7 (7: 9: 9: 11) rounds, 3 (3: 3: 5: 5) foll alt rounds and 2 (4: 3: 6: 7) 4th rounds. 190 (226: 218: 242: 274) sts total; 88 (106: 102: 114: 130) sts each for Front and Back and 7 sts per steek.

You should have just completed Row 99 (113: 111: 137: 155) of chart.

Continue straight until you have completed Row 113 (127: 125: 141: 161) of chart for women's version or Row 123 (139: 137: 153: 173) of chart for men's version.

Shape front neck

You will now shape the front neck. To do this, you will need to continue working back and forth in rows, turning at neck edge each time. While shaping the front neck, continue working steek across armholes, as well purling in pattern on WS rows and stranding yarn not in use across WS of work.

WOMEN'S VERSION

Next Round: Work as set across steek, then pattern across next 30 (37: 33: 37: 43) sts for Left Front, cast off next 28 (32: 36: 40: 44) sts for front neck, pattern until you have 30 (37: 33: 37: 43) sts for Right Front on right needle after cast-off sts, work as set across steek, pattern across 88 (106: 102: 114: 130) sts for Back. 162 (194: 182: 202: 230) sts total; 30 (37: 33: 37: 43) sts each for Left and Right Fronts, 7 sts per steek and 88 (106: 102: 114: 130) sts for Back.

Break yarn.

With RS facing, rejoin yarn to Right Front at neck edge (left front as you are looking at your work).

Pattern continues overleaf

Cast off 4 sts at the beginning of the next 2 rows, 3 sts at the beginning of the following 2 rows and 2 sts at the beginning of following 2 rows, working across steeks as before. 144 (176: 164: 184: 212) sts total; 21 (28: 24: 28: 34) sts each for Left and Right Fronts, 7 sts per steek and 88 (106: 102: 114: 130) sts for Back.

Dec Row (RS): K1, ssk, pattern to last 3 sts, k2tog, k1. 2 sts dec'd.

Dec Row (WS): P1, p2tog, pattern to last 3 sts, p2tog tbl, p1. 2 sts dec'd.

Decrease 1 st at each neck edge as set on next 1 (3: 1: 3: 3) rows. 138 (166: 158: 174: 202) sts total; 18 (23: 21: 23: 29) sts each for Left and Right Fronts, 7 sts per steek and 88 (106: 102: 114: 130) sts for Back.

Work 1 row straight.

Repeat RS Dec Row again. 2 sts dec'd.

Repeat last 2 rows another 0 (2: 1: 0: 2) times. 136 (160: 154: 172: 196) sts total; 17 (20: 19: 22: 26) sts each for Left and Right Fronts, 7 sts per steek and 88 (106: 102: 114: 130) sts for Back.

Work 10 (8: 10: 12: 12) rows straight in pattern, ending after a RS row. You should have completed Row 135 (153: 149: 167: 191) of chart.

You will now cast off steeks and work Back and Fronts separately.

Next row (WS): Pattern across 17 (20: 19: 22: 26) Left Front sts to steek, cast off next 7 steek sts, pattern until you have 88 (106: 102: 114: 130) sts for Back on your right needle, cast off next 7 steek sts, pattern across 17 (20: 19: 22: 26) Right Front sts to end, noting that the first of these sts will already be on your right needle after casting off. 122 (146: 140: 158: 182) sts total; 17 (20: 19: 22: 26) sts each for Right and Left Fronts and 88 (106: 102: 114: 130) sts for Back.

Shape right front shoulder

Turn and continue on these last 17 (20: 19: 22: 26) Right Front sts only.

Now work another 17 rows straight (all charts), but when you work these rows, work TOP DOWN through the previous rows of the chart before the row you worked when casting off

the steeks. This means that the motif you've just worked will be mirrored and that the top edge of the front shoulder will join to the correct row of the pattern where it meets the back shoulder.

Leave on a stitch holder or spare needle. Break yarn.

Shape left front shoulder

Rejoin yarn with RS facing to 17 (20: 19: 22: 26) Left Front sts.

Work straight as for first shoulder.

Back

With RS facing, rejoin yarn to the 88 (106: 102: 114: 130) Back sts.

Next row (RS): Pattern 20 (23: 22: 25: 29) sts for Right Back, cast off next 48 (60: 58: 64: 72) sts for back neck, pattern 20 (23: 22: 25: 29) sts for Left Back to end, noting that the first of these sts will already be on your right needle after casting off.

Turn and continue on these last 20 (23: 22: 25: 29) Left Back sts only.

Shape left back neck

Dec Row (WS): Pattern to last 3 sts, p2tog tbl, p1. 1 st dec'd.

Dec Row (RS): K1, ssk, pattern to end. 1 st dec'd.

Repeat WS Dec Row once more. 17 (20: 19: 22: 26) sts.

Work straight in pattern for another 2 rows, ending after a WS row.

Leave sts on a holder or waste yarn.

Shape right back neck

With WS facing, rejoin yarn to the rem 20 (23: 22: 25: 29) Right Back sts.

Dec Row (WS): P1, p2tog, pattern to end. 1 st dec'd.

Dec Row (RS): Pattern to last 3 sts, k2tog, k1. 1 st dec'd.

Repeat WS Dec Row once more. 17 (20: 19: 22: 26) sts.

Work straight in pattern for another 2 rows, ending after a WS row.

42

Leave sts on a holder or waste yarn.

MEN'S VERSION

Next round: Work as set across steek, then pattern across next 34 (43: 41: 47: 53) sts for Left Front, cast off next 20 (20: 20: 20: 24) sts for Front neck, pattern until you have 34 (43: 41: 47: 53) sts for Right Front on right needle after cast-off sts, work as set across steek, pattern across 88 (106: 102: 114: 130) sts for Back. 170 (206: 198: 222: 250) sts; 34 (43: 41: 47: 53) sts for Left and Right Front, 88 (106: 102: 114: 130) sts for Back and 7 sts per steek.

Break yarn.

With RS facing, rejoin yarn to Right Front at neck edge (left front as you are looking at your work).

Cast off 4 sts at the beginning of the next 2 rows, 3 sts at the beginning of the following 2 rows and 2 sts at the beginning of following 2 rows, working across steeks as before. 152 (188: 180: 204: 232) sts; 25 (34: 32: 38: 44) sts each for Left and Right Fronts, 7 sts per steek and 88 (106: 102: 114: 130) sts for Back.

Dec Row (RS): K1, ssk, pattern to last 3 sts, k2tog, k1. 2 sts dec'd.

Dec Row (WS): P1, p2tog, pattern to last 3 sts, p2tog tbl, p1. 2 sts dec'd.

Decrease 1 st at each neck edge as set on next 1 (3: 1: 3: 1) rows. 146 (178: 174: 194: 226) sts; 22 (29: 29: 33: 41) sts each for Left and Right Front, 7 sts per steek and 88 (106: 102: 114: 130) sts for Back.

Size XL only

Work 1 row straight.

Repeat RS Dec Row again. 2 sts dec'd

Repeat last 2 rows once more. 222 sts; 39 sts each for Left and Right Front, 7 sts per steek and 130 sts for Back.

All sizes

Work 2 (4: 2: 2: 4) rows straight in pattern, ending after a RS row. You should have completed Row 135 (153: 149: 167: 191) of chart.

You will now cast off steeks and work Back and fronts separately.

Next row (WS): Pattern across 22 (29: 29: 33: 39) Left Front sts to steek, cast off next 7 steek sts, pattern until you have 88 (106: 102: 114: 130) sts for Back on your right needle, cast off next 7 steek sts, pattern across 22 (29: 29: 33: 39) Right Front sts to end, noting that the first of these sts will already be on your right needle after casting off. 132 (164: 160: 180: 208) sts; 22 (29: 29: 33: 39) sts each for Right and Left fronts and 88 (106: 102: 114: 130) sts for Back.

Shape right front shoulder

Turn and continue on these last 22 (29: 29: 33: 39) Right Front sts only.

Now work another 17 rows straight (all charts), but when you work these rows, work TOP DOWN through the previous rows of the chart before the row you worked when casting off the steeks. This means that the motif you've just worked will be mirrored and that the top edge of the front shoulder will join to the correct row of the pattern where it meets the back shoulder.

Leave on a stitch holder or spare needle. Break yarn.

Shape left front shoulder

Rejoin yarn with RS facing to 22 (29: 29: 33: 39) Left Front sts.

Work straight as for first shoulder.

Back

With RS facing, rejoin yarn to the 88 (106: 102: 114: 130) Back sts.

Next row (RS): Pattern 25 (32: 32: 36: 42) sts for Right Back, cast off next 38 (42: 38: 42: 46) sts for Back neck, pattern 25 (32: 32: 36: 42) sts for Left Back to end, noting that the first of these sts will already be on your right needle after casting off.

Turn and continue on these last 25 (32: 32: 36: 42) Left Back sts only.

Pattern continues overleaf

SLEEVELESS
ROUND-NECK VEST

Grey
colourway

☐	Knit
⬚	Pattern repeat
▨	123 Oxford
☐	122 Granite

NO. 25G BALLS NEEDED

COLOUR CODE	XS	S	M	L	XL
123 >	5	6	7	7	8
122 >	4	4	5	5	5

44

EXTRA SMALL

SMALL

MEDIUM

Shape left back neck

Dec Row (WS): Pattern to last 3 sts, p2tog tbl, p1. 1 st dec'd.

Dec Row (RS): K1, ssk, pattern to end. 1 st dec'd.

Repeat WS Dec Row once more. 22 (29: 29: 33: 39) sts.

Work straight in pattern for another 2 rows, ending after a WS row.

Leave sts on a holder or waste yarn.

Shape right back neck

With WS facing, rejoin yarn to the rem 25 (32: 32: 36: 42) Right Back sts.

Dec Row (WS): P1, p2tog, pattern to end. 1 st dec'd.

Dec Row (RS): Pattern to last 3 sts, k2tog, k1. 1 st dec'd.

Repeat WS Dec Row once more. 22 (29: 29: 33: 39) sts.

Work straight in pattern for another 2 rows, ending after a WS row.

Leave sts on a holder or waste yarn.

Finishing

WOMEN'S VERSION

With WS facing each other, and working from the armhole edge inwards, rejoin MC. Using Kitchener stitch, graft together the first 17 (20: 19: 22: 26) sts of Back together with the 17 (20: 19: 22: 26) sts of Left Shoulder, placing a waste yarn marker in this join as a reference point.

Repeat for Right Shoulder.

Pattern continues overleaf

SLEEVELESS
ROUND-NECK VEST

Traditional
Colourway

☐	Knit
☐	Pattern repeat
■	587 Madder
■	726 Prussian
▧	289 Gold
☐	104 Natural White

COLOUR CODE	NO. 25G BALLS NEEDED				
	XS	S	M	L	XL
587 >	5	6	7	7	8
726 >	3	3	4	4	4
289 >	3	3	4	4	4
104 >	4	4	5	6	6

EXTRA SMALL

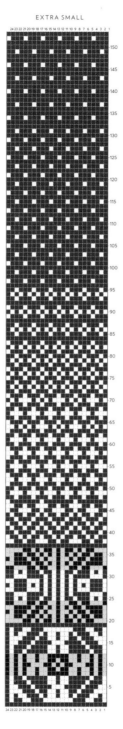

SMALL

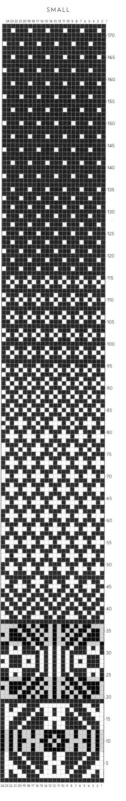

MEDIUM

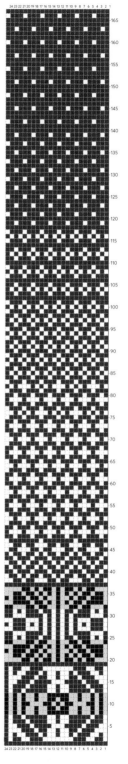

MEN'S VERSION

With WS facing each other, and working from the armhole edge inwards, rejoin MC. Using Kitchener stitch, graft together the first 22 (29: 29: 33: 39) sts of Back together with the 22 (29: 29: 33: 39) sts of Left Shoulder, placing a waste yarn marker in this join as a reference point.

Repeat for Right Shoulder.

WOMEN'S AND MEN'S VERSIONS

Lay garment flat so that the shoulder joins are sitting at back, and place a waste yarn marker at left and right armhole edges of the new natural fold at the top of the shoulder.

Armhole edging

Crochet 2 chains up the steek 1 st either side of the central stitch.

Carefully cut open steek with a pair of small sharp scissors, by cutting through the central stitch. Fold back, using the purl stitch as a guide, and catch down the edges to the inside of the garment.

With RS facing, MC and smaller DPNs or short circular needles, and beginning at centre of underarm, pick up and knit 128 (152: 152: 164: 188) sts around armhole edge, picking up 1 st for every cast-off st at underarm and then approx 8 sts for every 10 rows around armhole, picking up through the last garment stitch before the folded-back purl stitch.

Rib Round: *K2, p2; rep from * to end of round.

Repeat Rib Round another 7 times.

Cast off in rib.

Pattern continues overleaf

SLEEVELESS
ROUND-NECK VEST

Ombre
Colourway

☐	Knit
[ ]	Pattern repeat
■	727 Admiral Navy
■	168 Clyde Blue
■	134 Blue Danube
☐	104 Natural White
■	578 Rust
■	478 Amber

COLOUR CODE	NO. 25G BALLS NEEDED				
	XS	S	M	L	XL
727 >	5	6	7	7	8
168 >	3	3	4	4	4
134 >	3	3	4	4	4
104 >	2	3	3	3	3
587 >	1	1	1	1	1
487 >	1	1	1	1	1

EXTRA SMALL

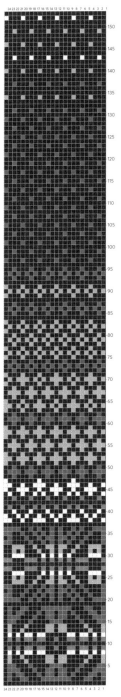

SMALL

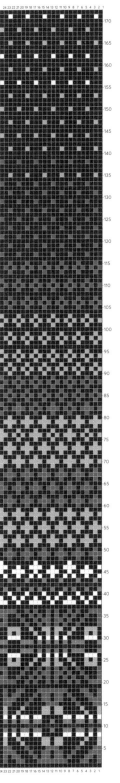

MEDIUM

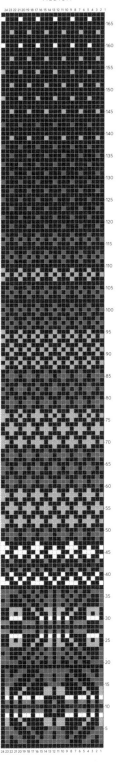

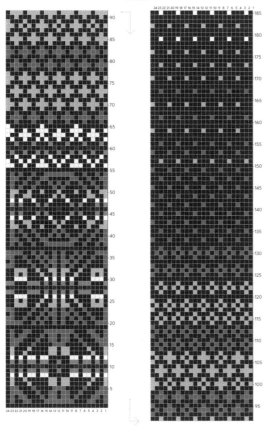

Neck edging

WOMEN'S VERSION

With RS facing, MC and smaller DPNs or short circular needles, and beginning at left shoulder join waste yarn marker, pick up and knit 35 (35: 36: 35: 40) sts up Left Back shoulder and down Left Front neck edge, 28 (32: 36: 40: 44) sts across Front neck, 35 (35: 36: 35: 40) sts up Right Front neck edge and down Right Back shoulder, and 58 (70: 68: 74: 82) sts around Back neck edge across Back neck shapings and centre back neck sts. 156 (172: 176: 184: 206) sts.

MEN'S VERSION

With RS facing, MC and smaller DPNs or short circular needles, and beginning at left shoulder join waste yarn marker, pick up and knit 25 (30: 36: 25: 30) sts up Left Back shoulder and down Left Front neck edge, 20 (20: 20: 20: 24) sts across Front neck, 25 (30: 36: 25: 30) sts up Right Front

neck edge and down Right Back shoulder, and 48 (52: 48: 52: 56) sts around Back neck edge across Back neck shapings and centre back neck sts. 118 (132: 140: 122: 140) sts.

WOMEN'S AND MEN'S VERSIONS

Rib Round: *K2, p2; rep from * to end of round.

Repeat Rib Round another 7 times.

Cast off in rib, casting off fairly firmly around curved sections to prevent edges from flaring out.

Weave in ends and block to measurements given at the beginning of the pattern.

PONCHO

This design came from a happy mistake when designing a conventional poncho. The prototype came up too big and Marie, my head designer, decided to leave half unsewn, turn it 45 degrees and make the neck into an armhole. The result is an asymmetrical design which has the practical benefit of making carrying a bag on your elbow easier.

This page: Poncho knitted by Melanie Matt
Opposite: Swimming at Gunglesund
Poncho knitted by Melanie Matt

50

	XS/S	M/L	XL
To fit chest circumference (approx)	81–91cm 32–36in	96.5–107cm 38–42in	112–122cm 44–48in
Width at lower edge	67.5cm 26½in	69cm 27¼in	71.5cm 28in
Length to side neck from side opening	49.5cm 19½in	50cm 19¾in	51cm 20in
Side edging depth	64cm 25¼in	71cm 28in	80cm 31½in
Neck width	24cm 9½in	27cm 10½in	29cm 11¼in
Neck edging depth	3.5cm 1¼in	4cm 1½in	4cm 1½in
Armhole depth	14.5cm 5½in	16cm 6¼in	17.5cm 7in
Armhole width	6cm 2½in	7.5cm 3in	8.5cm 3¼in
Armhole edging depth	3.5cm 1¼in	4cm 1½in	3.5cm 1¼in

YARN

Jamieson's of Shetland, Shetland Spindrift 4ply weight, 100% Shetland wool, 105m (115yd) per 25g ball

Grey colourway
- **15** × 123 Oxford **MC**
- **15** × 122 Granite

Traditional colourway
- **15** × 587 Madder **MC**
- **6** × 726 Prussian
- **6** × 289 Gold
- **12** × 104 Natural White

Admiral colourway
- **24** × 727 Admiral Navy **MC**
- **9** × 168 Clyde Blue
- **9** × 134 Blue Danube
- **6** × 104 Natural White
- **3** × 578 Rust
- **3** × 478 Amber

TENSION

All the garments in this book have been created using different tensions depending on the size being knitted. This allows us to offer a variety of sizes without having to use partial repeats of the 24-stitch patterns.

You may need to experiment with needle sizes to achieve the required tension for your size. If you've achieved the correct stitch tension but your round/row tension is wrong, try changing needle size by the smallest increment available, as this will often be enough to alter your round/row tension without compromising your stitch tension.

If you find you can only achieve stitch tension but not round/row tension, remember that you can still block out a small difference in round/row tension. Always block your swatch in the same way that you will block the finished garment. See page 141 for blocking instructions.

Sizes XS/S and XL only
30 stitches and 34 rounds/rows to 10cm (4in), measured over blocked stranded colourwork, using 2.75mm (US 2, UK 12) needles.

If necessary, change your needle size to achieve the stated tension.

Size M/L only
27 stitches and 30 rounds/rows to 10cm (4in), measured over blocked stranded colourwork, using 3.25mm (US 3, UK 10) needles.

If necessary, change your needle size to achieve the stated tension.

NEEDLES & NOTIONS

Circular needle for the required tension for your size, 100cm (40in) long

A circular needle one size smaller than that used to achieve stated tension, for edgings, 100cm (40in) long

1 set double-pointed needles for the required tension

1 stitch marker plus 15 (15: 19) stitch markers, in a contrasting colour (optional)

Tapestry needle.

Small crochet hook.

Needle and polyester or wool thread.

Small sharp scissors.

NOTES

When working colourwork sections, strand colour not in use evenly across the wrong side of your work.

All chart rows should be read from right to left.

Lower edge opening is made by casting on for a steek after the initial edging rows are worked. Neck opening and armhole are made by casting off body stitches and then casting on for steeks.

All steeks are cut open later and stitched down.

Note that this design is asymmetrical and that there will be a slight slouch on the higher side of the neck.

INSTRUCTIONS

With MC, and smaller circular needles, cast on 385 (385: 481) sts. Do not join.

Next row (Row 2 of chart) (WS): Purl.

Next row (Row 3 of chart) (RS): Knit.

This edging is worked by using two separate strands of the same colour, alternating them across each row. In this way, you create a single-colour form of stranded colourwork, which has the same tension as the colourwork section you will work later work.

For the second strand, pull from the centre of the ball.

If you are following the chart, you will see a symbol indicating when to use the second strand, given here as kwss.

Next row (Row 4 of chart) (WS): *P1, pwss; rep from * to last st, p1.

Next row (Row 5 of chart) (RS): *Kwss, k1; rep from * to last st, k1.

Repeat last 2 rows another 2 times.

Next row (Row 10 of chart) (WS): Purl.

Next row (Row 11 of chart) (RS): Knit to end. Do not turn.

Follow written pattern below and refer to chart for colourwork placement only.

When working steek across remaining body stitches, use two colours, alternating every other stitch to create a chequerboard or stripe effect, and using MC for first and last stitch of steek.

Steeks should always be worked as follows: P1, k9, p1.

Purling at the edges of the steek allows you to fold back the edge easily later.

Body

Change to larger circular needles.

Cast on 11 sts for lower edge opening steek using backwards loop method and join for working in the round. 396 (396, 492) sts total; 385 (385, 481) sts for the body and 11 sts for the steek.

Work lower edge steek, then, beginning with Row 12 of the chart, work colourwork section, repeating the 24-st pattern 16 (16: 20) times per round, and then work last st of chart, placing markers every 24 sts to denote repeats if desired on first of these rounds.

Continue in colourwork pattern until you have completed Round 167 (149: 173).

Set neck steek

Next Round: Work lower edge steek, pattern 192 (192: 240) sts, cast off 1 st, pattern to end of round.

You will now cast on for steek across neck.

Next Round: Work lower edge steek, pattern 192 (192: 240) sts, then using the backward loop method and MC, cast on 11 sts across neck, pattern to end. 406 (406: 502) sts total; 192 (192: 240) sts each for Front and Back and 11 sts per steek.

Next Round: Work lower edge steek, pattern 192 (192: 240) sts to neck, p1, k9, p1 across neck steek, pattern 192 (192: 240) sts to end.

Continue working straight, keeping Front and Back pattern and steeks correct, until you have completed Round 229 (207: 243).

Set top of armhole steek

Next Round: Cast off the 11 lower edge steek sts, cast off 43 (43: 53) sts for armhole, noting that the first of these sts will already be on your right needle after casting off steek, pattern 149 (149: 187) sts to neck steek, work neck steek, pattern 149 (149: 187) sts, cast off 43 (43: 53) sts for armhole. DO NOT TURN. 309 (309: 385) sts total; 149 (149: 187) sts each for Front and Back and 11 sts for neck steek.

Slip last st worked back to left needle (this st was on right needle after finishing cast off).

Next Round: Using MC and the backward loop method, cast on 7 steek sts for side for armhole steek, pattern 149 (149: 187) sts to neck steek, work neck steek, pattern to end. 316 (316: 392) sts total; 7 sts for armhole steek, 149 (149: 187) sts each for Front and Back and 11 sts for neck steek.

Next Round: P1, k5, p1 across armhole steek, pattern to neck steek, work neck steek, pattern to end.

Continue working straight, keeping Front and Back pattern and steeks correct, until you have completed Round 249 (229: 271).

Next Round: Cast off the 7 armhole steek sts, pattern to neck steek, cast off the 11 neck steek sts, pattern to end. 298 (298: 374) sts total; 149 (149: 187) sts each for Front and Back.

Finishing

Break yarn.

Use MC to join the Front side edging sts to the Back side edging sts, either by using the three-needle cast-off method with RS facing each other or by grafting them together with WS facing each other.

Pattern continues overleaf

Steek finishing

You will use the same method to finish all three steeks.

Crochet 2 chains up the steek, 1 st either side of the central stitch.

Carefully cut open steek with a pair of small sharp scissors, by cutting through the central stitch. Fold back, using the purl stitch as a guide, and catch down the edges to the inside of the garment.

Armhole edging

With RS facing, using MC and smaller circular needles, and beginning at side neck edge of front opening, pick up and knit 43 (43: 53) sts across front armhole, 16 (18: 22) sts up front armhole, 17 (19: 23) sts down back armhole and 43 (43: 53) sts across back armhole. DO NOT JOIN. 119 (123: 151) sts.

Beginning with a WS (purl) row, work 2 rows in st st.

Row 1 (WS): *P1, pwss; rep from * to last st, p1.

Row 2: *Kwss, k1; rep from * to last st, kwss.

Repeat Rows 1–2 twice more and then Row 1 once more.

Work 3 rows in st st, ending after a RS row.

Cast off knitwise on WS.

54

Grey colourway

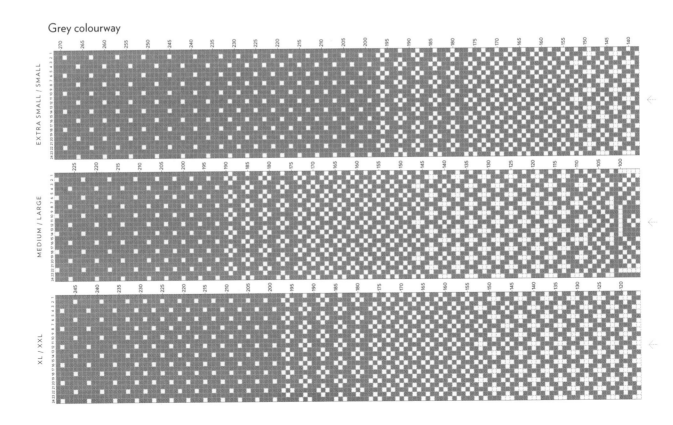

Neck edging

With RS facing, using MC and smaller double-pointed needles, and beginning at the inner edge of the neck opening, pick up and knit 66 (65: 79) sts along one neck edge and 66 (65: 79) sts along the other. Join to work in the round, and place marker for beginning of round. 132 (130: 158) sts.

Work 2 rounds in st st.

Round 1: *K1, kwss; rep from * to end.
Round 2: *Kwss, k1; rep from * to end.
Repeat Rounds 1–2 another 2 (2: 3) times and then Round 1 once more.

Work 3 rounds in st st.

Cast off purlwise on RS.

Lower edge opening finishing

With RS facing, using MC and smaller circular needles, pick up evenly, 4 sts every 5 rows, along lower edge, ending with an odd number of sts.

Work as for Rows 2 to 11 of Body edging worked after cast-on at beginning of pattern.

Cast off.

Weave in ends and block to measurements given at the beginning of the pattern.

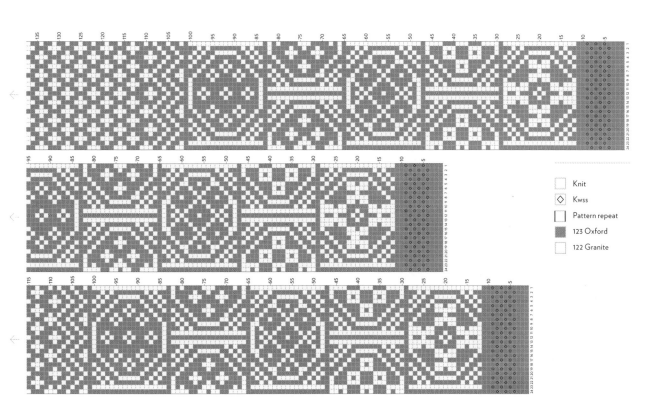

Knit
Kwss
Pattern repeat
123 Oxford
122 Granite

Poncho – Traditional Colourway

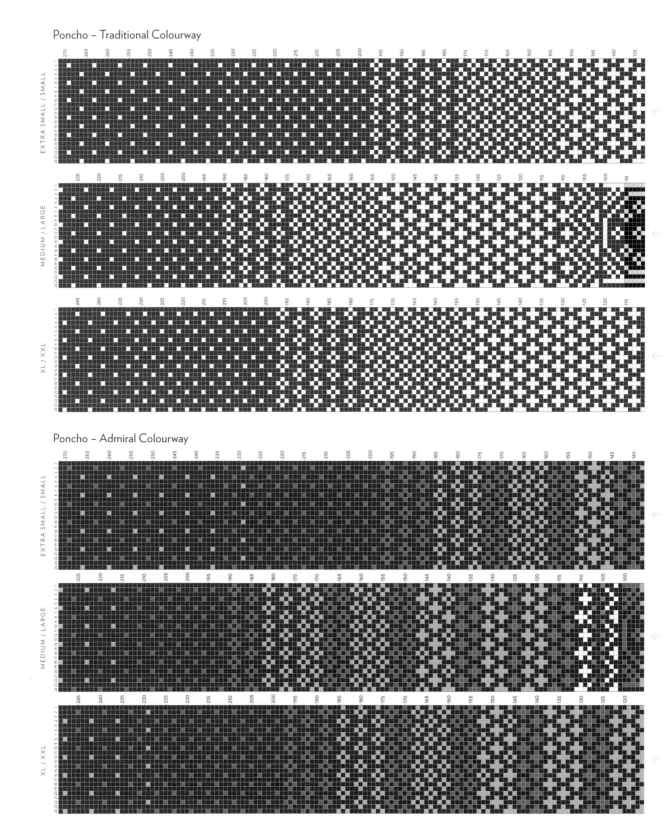

Poncho – Admiral Colourway

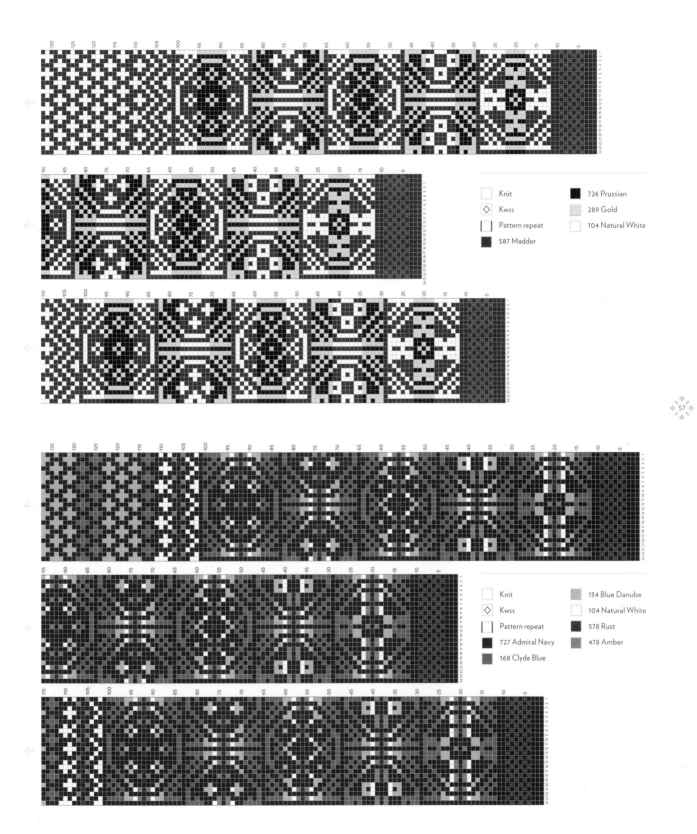

Knit

Kwss

Pattern repeat

587 Madder

726 Prussian

289 Gold

104 Natural White

Knit

Kwss

Pattern repeat

727 Admiral Navy

168 Clyde Blue

134 Blue Danube

104 Natural White

578 Rust

478 Amber

PLAYING WITH BACKGROUNDS

Studying museum pieces and the work of
Annie Thomson, one of the oldest knitters
in Fair Isle, helped me to understand
the use of motifs and colour to develop
a way of expressing myself through Fair
Isle knitting. It was like learning a new
language: first learning the motifs (words),
then creating visual patterns (sentences)
and finally adding colour (intonation).
Anne Sinclair, Annie's daughter and Fair
Isle's social historian, once showed me a
knitted piece from the George Waterston
Museum collection dating back to the
1860s where the Muckle Flooers appear
continuously through the piece, with only
one plain row in between bands of motifs
and regularly changing between two
colours in correlation to the background.
The background is a regular repetition of
stripes in two colours.

In this group of projects I explore the
foreground/background relationship.
I use the motifs as an independent lace-like
piece of knitting superimposed onto a
background of regular 'bands' of colour
that change in size, number of colours
and rhythm.

Malcom's Head, Taft Croft and Nedder Taft

WRIST WARMERS

There is no better way of testing a design than knitting a small swatch, but better still is making something out of it. I often knit wrist warmers as a way of testing designs while still making something useful. They are not only stylish, but also an essential item to protect your wrists from the cold. This is an ideal project if you are new to colourwork.

SIZE	S / M
To fit hand circumference measured around knuckles	15–22cm 6–8½in
Finished circumference	18cm 7in
Finished height	25cm 9¾in

YARN

Jamieson's of Shetland, Shetland Spindrift
4ply weight, 100% Shetland wool, 105m (115yd) per 25g ball

Natural colourway
- 1 × 101 Natural Black **MC**
- 1 × 104 Natural White

Traditional colourway
- 1 × 101 Natural Black **MC**
- 1 × 289 Gold
- 1 × 587 Madder
- 1 × 726 Prussian
- 1 × 104 Natural White

Ombre colourway
- 1 × 727 Admiral Navy
- 1 × 105 Eesit
- 1 × 104 Natural White
- 1 × 478 Amber
- 1 × 578 Rust
- 1 × 168 Clyde Blue
- 1 × 136 Teviot
- 1 × 134 Blue Danube

Above: Wrist warmers knitted by Anna Mäkilä
Opposite: Feeding the cats at Taft Croft
Wrist warmers knitted by Anna Mäkilä

TENSION

27 stitches and 30 rounds to 10cm (4in), measured over blocked, stranded colourwork, using 3.25mm (US 3, UK 10) needles.

If necessary, change your needle size to achieve the stated tension.

NEEDLES & NOTIONS

1 set 3.25mm (US 3, UK 10) double-pointed needles or long circular needle for magic loop method

Tapestry needle

1 stitch marker

NOTES

When working colourwork sections, strand colour not in use evenly across the back (wrong side) of your work.

All chart rounds should be read from right to left.

INSTRUCTIONS

With MC, cast on 48 sts using the long-tail or twisted German cast-on method.

Join to work in the round, being careful not to twist. Place marker for beginning of round.

Wrist warmers can be worked entirely from chart, repeating the 24-stitch pattern twice per round. If this is your preferred method, read the section on Lower Edging before working Rounds 2–9 and the section on Upper Edging before working Rounds 67–74. Follow chart until you have completed Round 75, then cast off purlwise.

Alternatively, follow written pattern below and refer to chart for colourwork section only.

Lower edging

Round 1: Knit to end of round.

This edging is now worked by using two separate strands of the same colour, alternating them across each round. In this way, you create a single-colour form of stranded colourwork, which will prevent the top edge of the wrist warmers from rolling over while remaining at the same tension as the colourwork section you will work next.

For the second strand, pull from the centre of the ball.

If you are following the chart, you will see a symbol indicating when to use the second strand, given here as kwss.

Round 2: *K1, kwss; rep from * to end of round.
Round 3: *Kwss, k1; rep from * to end of round.

Repeat last 2 rounds another 3 times, changing colour as indicated on chart.

Continue with one strand of MC on next round.

Main section

Rounds 10–66: Knit, following chart.

Upper edging

Round 67: Using colour shown on chart, *kwss, k1; rep from * to end of round.

Round 68: *K1, kwss; rep from * to end of round.

Repeat last 2 rounds another 3 times, changing colour as indicated on chart.

Continue with one strand of MC for Natural and Traditional colourways, or 134 Blue Danube for Ombre colourway, on next round.

Round 75: Knit to end of round. Cast off purlwise.

Finishing

Weave in ends and block to measurements given at the beginning of the pattern. Repeat pattern for second wrist warmer.

Natural
colourway

☐ Knit

◇ Kwss

■ 101 Natural Black

☐ 104 Natural White

☐ Centre stitch

Traditional
colourway

Knit
◇ Kwss
■ 101 Natural Black
▨ 289 Gold
▧ 587 Madder
▩ 726 Prusian Blue
☐ 104 Natural White
☐ Centre stitch

Ombre colourway

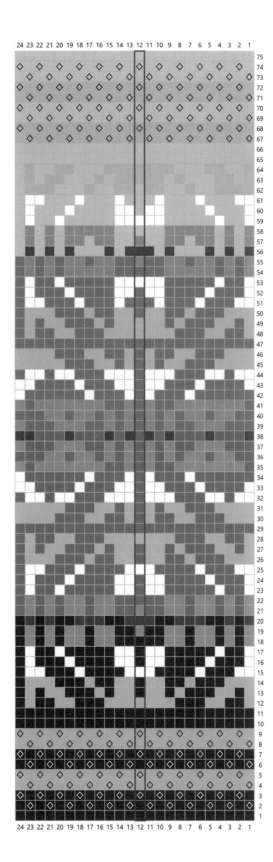

- ☐ Knit
- ◇ Kwss
- ■ 727 Admiral Navy
- ▨ 105 Eesit
- ☐ 104 Natural White
- ▨ 478 Amber
- ■ 578 Rust
- ▨ 168 Clyde Blue
- ▨ 136 Teviot
- ▨ 134 Blue Danube
- ☐ Centre stitch

KEP HAT

Keps are the traditional hats worn by Fair Isle fishermen, and like the Fair Isle knitting technique and motifs, no one really knows exactly where they came from. Similar hats are found all over the Baltic countries and specially in the Netherlands. Shetland was an important port and it was visited by Dutch merchants and fishing vessels for many centuries.

Above: Hat knitted by Maj Corio
Opposite: Preparing a fishing line
Hat knitted by Patricia Philbin

SIZE

		S	M	L
To fit head circumference (approx)		47cm 18½in	55cm 21¾in	64cm 25¼in
Actual hat circumference at brim		44.5cm 17½in	53cm 21in	62cm 24½in
Kep Hat length	Brim unfolded	47cm 18½in	Brim folded	39cm 15¼in

YARN

Jamieson's of Shetland, Shetland Spindrift
4ply weight, 100% Shetland wool, 105m (115yd) per 25g ball

Natural colourway
- ● **2** × 101 Natural Black **MC**
- ○ **1** × 104 Natural White

Traditional colourway
- ● **2** × 101 Natural Black **MC**
- ● **1** × 289 Gold
- ● **1** × 587 Madder
- ● **1** × 726 Prussian
- ○ **1** × 104 Natural White

Ombre colourway
- ● **2** × 727 Admiral Navy
- ● **1** × 105 Eesit
- ○ **1** × 122 Granite
- ○ **1** × 104 Natural White
- ● **1** × 1190 Burnt Umber
- ● **1** × 168 Clyde Blue
- ● **1** × 136 Teviot
- ● **1** × 134 Blue Danube

TENSION

27 stitches and 30 rounds to 10cm (4in), measured over blocked stranded colourwork, using 3.25mm (US 3, UK 10) needles.

If necessary, change your needle size to achieve the stated tension.

NEEDLES & NOTIONS

1 set 2.75mm (US 2, UK 12) double-pointed needles or long circular needle for magic loop method

1 set 3.25mm (US 3, UK 10) double-pointed needles or long circular needle for magic loop method

1 stitch marker plus 4 (5: 6) stitch markers, in a contrasting colour (optional)

Tapestry needle

NOTES

When working colourwork sections, strand colour not in use loosely across the back (wrong side) of your work.

All chart rows should be read from right to left.

INSTRUCTIONS

With MC and smaller needles, make a slip knot and place on needle as the first st, leaving a long tail for casting on. Cast on 1 st using the long-tail cast-on method, then cast on 2 sts using the twisted German cast-on method. *Cast on 2 sts using the long-tail cast-on method, cast on 2 sts using the twisted German cast-on method; repeat from * until there are 120 (144: 168) sts on the needle. Join to work in the round, being careful not to twist. Place marker for beginning of round.

Hat can be worked entirely from chart, repeating the 24-stitch pattern 5 (6: 7) times per round. If this is your preferred method, follow chart to end, changing to larger needles when rib is complete, and then follow Round 138 as written below – this round is not shown on the chart.

Alternatively, follow written pattern below and refer to chart for colourwork sections only.

Important note

Whether you follow chart or written pattern, hat should be turned inside out once while working, after Round 24, to turn it back to face the correct way. This is to ensure that the colourwork on the kep brim faces right side out when worn. To avoid a hole when turning work inside out and changing direction, wrap and turn around the last stitch of Round 23.

Brim

Rib Round: *K2, p2; rep from * to end of round.

Work Rib Round another 3 times.

Change to larger needles.

Round 5: Knit to end of round.

Work first colourwork section, following Rows 6–22 of chart, repeating the 24-stitch pattern 5 (6: 7) times per round and placing contrast markers every 24 sts to denote repeats, if desired, on first of these rounds.

Round 23: With MC only, knit to end of round.

Round 24: With MC only, purl to last st, wrap and turn.

Turn work inside out, so that the right side of the colourwork section is facing inwards. You will now be working in the opposite direction.

Alt Rib Round: *P2, k2; rep from * to end of round.

Work Alt Rib Round another 20 times.

Main section

Work second colourwork section, following Rows 46–123 of chart.

Colourwork sections are now complete.

Round 124: With MC for Natural and Traditional colourways, or 134 Blue Danube for Ombre colourway, knit to end of round, removing any pattern repeat markers as you come to them.

Crown decreases

Round 125: *K6, k2tog; rep from * to end. 15 (18: 21) sts dec'd. 105 (126: 147) sts rem.

Round 126: Knit to end of round.

Round 127: *K5, k2tog; rep from * to end. 15 (18: 21) sts dec'd. 90 (108: 126) sts rem.

Round 128: Knit to end of round.

Round 129: *K4, k2tog; rep from * to end. 15 (18: 21) sts dec'd. 75 (90: 105) sts rem.

Round 130: Knit to end of round.

Round 131: *K3, k2tog; rep from * to end. 15 (18: 21) sts dec'd. 60 (72: 84) sts rem.

Round 132: Knit to end of round.

Round 133: *K2, k2tog; rep from * to end. 15 (18: 21) sts dec'd. 45 (54: 63) sts rem.

Round 134: Knit to end of round.

Round 135: *K1, k2tog; rep from * to end. 15 (18: 21) sts dec'd. 30 (36: 42) sts rem.

Round 136: Knit to end of round.

Round 137: *K2tog; rep from * to end. 15 (18: 21) sts dec'd. 15 (18: 21) sts rem.

Round 138 (not shown on chart): K1 (0: 1), *k2tog; rep from * to end. 7 (9: 10) sts dec'd. 8 (9: 11) sts rem.

Finishing

Break yarn and thread through rem sts. Pull tight to fasten.

Weave in ends and block to measurements given at the beginning of the pattern.

Fold brim back at Round 24 and catch in place if desired with whip stitches.

Tassel

Wind 2, 3 or 4 strands of contrasting yarn lengthways around an 11cm (4^1/$_4$in) piece of thick card or a slim book.

If using 2 strands, wrap card 40 times.

If using 3 strands, wrap card 25 times.

If using 4 strands, wrap card 20 times.

Carefully cut the strands at one end, and at the other end use a strand of yarn to secure the tassel. Make a cord by twisting 2 strands of yarn and then use this to tie the secured centre with a knot. Wrap another strand of yarn around the tassel about 4cm (1^1/$_2$in) from the centre, creating a round-top ball. Attach the tassel to the crown of the hat using the two cord ends, and weave in the ends on the inside around the closed stitches.

Natural colourway

Knit
Purl
K2tog
101 Natural Black
104 Natural White

Traditional colourway

Knit
Purl
K2tog
101 Natural Black
289 Gold
587 Madder
726 Prussian
104 Natural White

Ombre colourway

Knit
Purl
K2tog
727 Admiral Navy
105 Eesit
122 Granite
104 Natural White
1190 Burnt Umber
168 Clyde Blue
136 Teviot
134 Blue Danube

71

ROUND SCARF

The round scarf was designed with practicality in mind – there are no tassels, no dangling ends, and it is quick and easy to put on. It is the perfect garment to display most of the traditional Muckle Flooers motifs that were used on Fair Isle garments as early as or before the 18th century.

SIZE	ONE SIZE
Finished circumference	145cm 57in
Finished height	36cm 14in

YARN

Jamieson's of Shetland,
Shetland Spindrift 4ply weight,
100% Shetland wool,
105m (115yd) per 25g ball

Natural colourway
- **5 ×** 101 Natural Black **MC**
- **5 ×** 104 Natural White

Traditional colourway
- **1 ×** 101 Natural Black **MC**
- **1 ×** 587 Madder
- **1 ×** 289 Gold
- **1 ×** 726 Prussian
- **2 ×** 104 Natural White

Ombre colourway
- **1 ×** 727 Admiral Navy
- **1 ×** 168 Clyde Blue
- **1 ×** 136 Teviot
- **1 ×** 134 Blue Danube
- **1 ×** 122 Granite
- **1 ×** 105 Eesit
- **1 ×** 478 Amber
- **1 ×** 578 Rust

Opposite: Dry stone wall building at Taft Croft
Scarf knitted by Jackie Kirkham
Below: Scarf knitted by Maj Corio

TENSION

27 stitches and 30 rows to 10cm (4in), measured over blocked stranded colourwork, using 3.25mm (US 3, UK 10) needles.

If necessary, change your needle size to achieve the stated tension.

NEEDLES & NOTIONS

1 pair 3.25mm (US 3, UK 10) straight needles

Smooth scrap yarn

Tapestry needle

NOTES

When working colourwork sections, strand colour not in use evenly across the back (wrong side) of your work.

Read RS rows from right to left and WS rows from left to right.

Note that the second repeat starts with a WS row.

On the first repeat, RS rows are odd and WS rows are even.

On the second repeat, RS rows are even and WS rows are odd.

INSTRUCTIONS

With scrap yarn and your preferred provisional cast-on method, cast on 97 sts.

Change to MC yarn.

Beginning with a knit row, work Rows 1–217 of chart twice in full, using the stranded st st technique. On each row, you will repeat the 24-stitch pattern four times and then work a final st to keep the pattern symmetrical.

When second repeat of chart is complete, leave working stitches live on one needle.

Break yarn, leaving a long tail, at least 1m (40in) long.

Undo the provisional cast-on and place live sts on second needle.

With WS facing, graft the two sets of sts together using Kitchener stitch and tapestry needle.

Finishing

Weave in ends and block to measurements given at the beginning of the pattern.

Natural colourway

- ☐ Knit
- ☐ Pattern repeat
- ■ 101 Natural Black
- ☐ 104 Natural White

Traditional
colourway

☐ Knit

▯ Pattern repeat

◼ 101 Natural Black

◼ 587 Madder

◻ 289 Gold

◼ 726 Prussian

☐ 104 Natural White

Ombre
colourway

Knit

Pattern repeat

727 Admiral Navy

105 Eesit

122 Granite

487 Amber

587 Rust

168 Clyde Blue

136 Teviot

134 Blue Danube

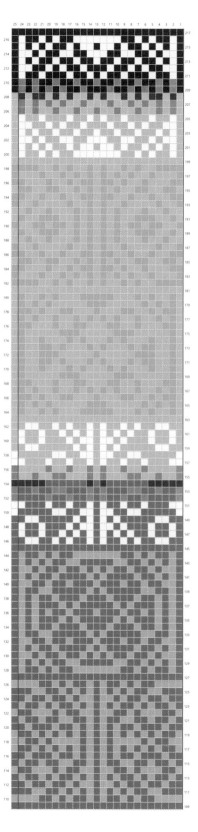

CREW NECK JUMPER

Crew necks are a wardrobe staple and
a symbol of comfort. This crew neck has
been designed with a modern fit and a
slightly wider neck, resulting in a more
casual garment. It is a great example of
adapting the scarf design for a garment.

This page: Jumper knitted by Suzanne Da Rosa
Opposite: Ditching at Taft Croft
Jumper knitted by Louise Bailey

YARN

Jamieson's of Shetland,
Shetland Spindrift
4ply weight,
100% Shetland wool,
105m (115yd) per 25g ball

Natural colourway

● 101 Natural Black **MC**

○ 104 Natural White

Traditional colourway

● 101 Natural Black **MC**

● 587 Madder

● 289 Gold

● 726 Prussian

○ 104 Natural White

Ombre colourway

● 727 Admiral Navy

● 168 Clyde Blue

● 136 Teviot

● 134 Blue Danube

● 106 Mooskit

● 105 Eesit

● 478 Amber

● 578 Rust

For number of balls of yarn required for
each size, refer to colourway charts.

SIZE	XS	S	M	L	XL
To fit chest circumference (approx)	76–84cm 30–33in	86–91cm 34–36in	97–102cm 38–40in	107–114cm 42–45in	117–122cm 46–48in
Actual chest circumference	89cm 35in	96cm 37¾in	107cm 42in	120cm 47¼in	128cm 50½in
Length to side shoulder	59.5cm 23½in	62cm 24½in	64cm 25¼in	66cm 26in	67.5cm 26½in
Armhole depth	19.5cm 7¾in	23cm 9in	24cm 9½in	26cm 10½in	26cm 10½in
Finished back neck width (Women's version)	15.5cm 6in	16cm 6¼in	16.5cm 6½in	18cm 7in	19cm 7¼in
Finished back neck width (Men's version)	10.5cm 4in	12cm 4¾in	11cm 4¼in	11.5cm 4½in	12.5cm 5in
Approx finished front neck depth (Women's version)	6.5cm 2½in	6.5cm 2½in	7.5cm 3in	7cm 2¾in	6.5cm 2½in
Approx finished front neck depth (Men's version)	6cm 2¼in	4cm 1½in	4.5cm 1¾in	4cm 1½in	4cm 1½in
Sleeve length (Women's version)	44cm 17¼in	44cm 17¼in	44cm 17¼in	43cm 17in	45cm 18¾in Natural & Traditional / 46cm 18in Ombre
Sleeve length (Men's version)	50cm 19¾in	50cm 19¾in	50cm 19¾in	49cm 19¼in	51cm 20in Natural & Traditional / 52cm 20½in Ombre
Cuff circumference	20.5cm 8in	21.5cm 8½in	23.5cm 9¼in	25.5cm 10in	26.5cm 10½in
Top sleeve circumference	30cm 11¾in	32cm 12½in	35cm 13¾in	38cm 15in	41cm 16in

TENSION

All the garments in this book have been created using different tensions depending on the size being knitted. This allows us to offer a variety of sizes without having to use partial repeats of the 24-stitch patterns.

You may need to experiment with needle sizes to achieve the required tension for your size. If you've achieved the correct stitch tension but your round/row tension is wrong, try changing needle size by the smallest increment available, as this will often be enough to alter your round/row tension without compromising your stitch tension.

If you find you can only achieve stitch tension but not round/row tension, remember that you can still block out a small difference in round/row tension. Always block your swatch in the same way that you will block the finished garment. See page 141 for blocking instructions.

Sizes XS and M only

27 stitches and 30 rounds/rows to 10cm (4in), measured over blocked stranded colourwork, using 3.25mm (US 3, UK 10) needles.

If necessary, change your needle size to achieve the stated tension.

Sizes S and XL only

30 stitches and 34 rounds/rows to 10cm (4in), measured over blocked stranded colourwork, using 2.75mm (US 2, UK 12) needles.

If necessary, change your needle size to achieve the stated tension.

Size L only

28 stitches and 32 rounds/rows to 10cm (4in), measured over blocked stranded colourwork, using 3mm (US 2/3, UK 11) needles.

If necessary, change your needle size to achieve the stated tension.

NEEDLES & NOTIONS

Circular needle two sizes below the size for the stated tension, 80cm (32in) long

Circular needle for the stated tension, 80cm (32in) long

1 set double-pointed needles for the stated tension

1 set double-pointed needles or shorter circular needle two sizes below the size for the stated tension

1 stitch marker plus 9 (11: 11: 13: 15) stitch markers, in a contrasting colour (optional)

Tapestry needle

Small crochet hook

Needle and polyester or wool thread

Small sharp scissors

NOTES

When working colourwork sections, strand colour not in use evenly across the back (wrong side) of your work.

All chart rows should be read from right to left when working in the round.

When working flat in rows, read odd-numbered rows from right to left and even-numbered rows from left to right.

Armholes are made by putting stitches on holders and then casting on for steeks, which are cut open later and stitched down.

INSTRUCTIONS

With MC and smaller circular needles, make a slip knot and place on needle as the first st, leaving a long tail for casting on. Cast on 1 st using the long-tail cast-on method, then cast on 2 sts using the twisted German cast-on method. *Cast on 2 sts using the long-tail cast-on method, cast on 2 sts using the twisted German cast-on method; repeat from * until there are 240 (288: 288: 336: 384) sts on the needle.

Pattern continues overleaf

Natural
colourway

Knit
Pattern repeat
■ 101 Natural Black
104 Natural White

NO. 25G BALLS NEEDED					
COLOUR CODE	XS	S	M	L	XL
101 >	7	8	9	10	10
104 >	8	9	10	12	12

81

Join to work in the round, being careful not to twist. Place marker for beginning of round.

Follow written pattern below and refer to chart for colourwork placement only.

Hem

Rib Round: *K2, p2; rep from * to end of round.

Repeat Rib Round another 11 (13: 11: 12: 13) times. Rib should measure 4cm (1¹/₂in) from cast-on edge.

Body

Change to larger circular needles.

Work colourwork section, beginning with row 55 for Natural and Traditional charts and row 37 (37: 37: 37: 54) for Ombre charts, repeating the 24-stitch pattern 10 (12: 12: 14: 16) times per round, placing markers every 24 sts to denote repeats if desired on the first of these rounds.

Continue in colourwork pattern until you have completed a total of 108 (120: 108: 114: 127) rounds of colourwork chart, ending last round 2 sts before end of round. This will be row 162 (174: 162: 168: 181) of Natural and Traditional charts and row 144 (156: 144: 150: 180) of Ombre charts.

Shape armholes and set steeks

Next Round: Cast off 5 sts, pattern until you have 115 (139: 139: 163: 187) sts on your needles, cast off the next 5 sts, pattern 115 (139: 139: 163: 187) sts to end of round, noting that the first of these sts will already be on your right needle after casting off. DO NOT BREAK YARN.

You will now cast on for steeks across both armholes.

Next Round: Using the backwards loop method and MC, cast on 7 sts across left underarm cast-off, pattern across 115 (139: 139: 163: 187) sts for Front, cast on 7 sts across right underarm cast-off, pattern across 115 (139: 139: 163: 187) sts for Back. 244 (292: 292: 340: 388) sts total; 115 (139: 139: 163: 187) sts each for Front and Back and 7 sts per steek.

When working steek stitches, use two colours, alternating every other stitch to create a chequerboard or stripe effect.

Steeks should always be worked as follows: P1, k5, p1.

Purling at the edges of the steek allows you to fold back the edge easily later.

Shape armholes

Dec Round: *P1, k5, p1 across steek, k1, ssk, knit to 3 sts before steek, k2tog, k1; rep from * once more. 4 sts dec'd.

Repeat Dec Round another 0 (0: 2: 2: 2) times. 240 (288: 280: 328: 376) sts; 113 (137: 133: 157: 181) sts each for Front and Back and 7 sts per steek.

Work 1 round straight.

Repeat Dec Round once more. 4 sts dec'd.

Repeat last 2 rounds another 5 (8: 9: 17: 22) times. 216 (252: 240: 256: 284) sts; 101 (119: 113: 121: 135) sts each for Front and Back and 7 sts per steek.

Sizes XS, S, M and L only

Work 3 rounds straight.

Repeat Dec Round once more. 4 sts dec'd.

Repeat last 4 rounds another 3 (3: 2: 0: -) times. 200 (236: 228: 252: -) sts; 93 (111: 107: 119: -) sts each for Front and Back and 7 sts per steek.

WOMEN'S VERSION ONLY

All sizes
Continue straight in pattern until you have completed 144 (162: 144: 162: 180) rounds from beginning of colourwork. Your last row will be row 198 (216: 198: 216: 234) of Natural and Traditional charts and row Row 180 (198: 180: 198: 233) of Ombre charts.

Shape front neck
You will now shape the front neck. To do this, you will need to work back and forth in rows, turning at neck edge each time. While shaping front neck, continue working steek across armholes, purling in pattern on WS rows and stranding yarn not in use across WS of work.

	NO. 25G BALLS NEEDED										
COLOUR CODE	XS	S	M	L	XL		COLOUR CODE	XS	S	M	L	XL
101 >	4	4	5	5	5		726 >	5	5	6	6	6
587 >	4	4	5	5	5		104 >	5	6	6	7	7
289 >	4	4	5	5	5							

Pattern continues overleaf

Traditional colourway

	Knit
	Pattern repeat
■	101 Natural Black
■	587 Madder

	289 Gold
■	726 Prussian
	104 Natural White

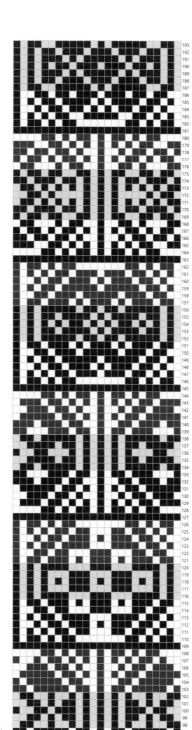

Next Round: Work steek, then pattern across next 23 (28: 29: 32: 36) sts for Left Front, pattern across next 47 (55: 49: 55: 63) sts for front neck and slip these sts onto waste yarn, pattern until you have 23 (28: 29: 32: 36) sts for Right Front on right needle after cast-off sts, work steek, pattern across 93 (111: 107: 119: 135) sts for Back. 153 (181: 179: 197: 221) sts; 23 (28: 29: 32: 36) sts each for Left and Right Fronts, 93 (111: 107: 119: 135) sts for Back and 7 sts for each steek.

Break yarn.

With WS facing, rejoin yarn to neck edge of Left Front.
Next row (WS): Maintaining pattern and steeks, work to end.
Dec Row (RS): K1, ssk, pattern to last 3 sts, k2tog, k1. 2 sts dec'd.
Work 1 row straight.
Repeat Dec Row. 2 sts dec'd.
Repeat last 2 rows another 2 times. 145 (173: 171: 189: 213) sts total; 19 (24: 25: 28: 32) sts each for Left and Right Fronts, 93 (111: 107: 119: 135) sts for Back and 7 sts per steek.

Natural and Traditional charts only
Work 9 (18: 18: 18: 18) rows straight, ending after a WS (RS: RS: RS: RS) row. You should have completed row 216 (243: 225: 243: 261) of charts.

Ombre charts only
Work 9 (18: 18: 17: 18) rows straight, ending after a WS (RS: RS: WS: RS) row. You should have completed row 198 (225: 207: 224: 260) of Ombre charts.

All versions
You will now cast off steeks and work Back and Fronts separately.
Next Row: Pattern 19 (24: 25: 28: 32) Front sts to steek, cast off next 7 steek sts, pattern until you have the 93 (111: 107: 119: 135) sts for Back on your right needle, cast off next 7 steek sts, pattern 19 (24: 25: 28: 32) Front sts to end, noting that the first of these sts will already be on your right needle after casting off.

Shape first front shoulder
Turn and continue on these last 19 (24: 25: 28: 32) Front sts only.
You will now work another 17 (8: 8: 8: 8) rows straight (all charts), but when you work these rows, work TOP DOWN through the previous rows of the chart before the row you worked when casting off the steeks. This means that the motif you've just worked will be mirrored and that the top edge of the front shoulder will join to the correct row of the pattern where it meets the back shoulder.
Work straight for set number of rows for your size as given above.

Leave on a stitch holder or spare needle. Break yarn.

Shape second front shoulder
Rejoin yarn with correct side facing for next row to 19 (24: 25: 28: 32) Front sts.
Work straight as for first shoulder for given number of rows for your chart and size.

Interim finishing
With WS facing each other, and working from the armhole edge inwards, rejoin MC. Using Kitchener stitch, graft together the first 19 (24: 25: 28: 32) sts of Back together with the 19 (24: 25: 28: 32) sts of Left Shoulder, slip next 55 (63: 57: 63: 71) sts to waste yarn, leaving 19 (24: 25: 28: 32) sts on left needle. Using Kitchener stitch, graft together these sts with 19 (24: 25: 28: 32) sts of Right Shoulder.
Lay garment flat so that the shoulder joins are sitting at back, and place a waste yarn marker at left and right armhole edges of the new natural fold at the top of the shoulder.

MEN'S VERSION ONLY

All sizes
Continue straight in pattern until you have completed 144 (171: 153: 171: 189) rounds from beginning of colourwork. This will be Row 198 (225: 207: 225: 243) of Natural and Traditional charts and Row 180 (207: 189: 207: 242) of Ombre charts.

Shape front neck
You will now shape the front neck. To do this, you will need to work back and forth in rows, turning at neck edge each time. While shaping front neck, continue working steek across armholes, purling in pattern on WS rows and stranding yarn not in use across WS of work.
Next round: Work steek, then pattern across next 29 (34: 35: 40: 45) sts for Left Front, pattern across next 35 (43: 37: 39: 45) sts for Front neck and slip these sts onto waste yarn, pattern until you have 29 (34: 35: 40: 45) sts for Right Front on right needle after cast-off sts, work steek, pattern across 93 (111: 107: 119: 135) sts for Back. 165 (193: 191: 213: 239) sts; 29 (34: 35: 40: 45) sts each for Left and Right Front, 93 (111: 107: 119: 135) sts for Back and 7 sts per steek.
Break yarn.
With WS facing, rejoin yarn to neck edge of Left Front.
Next row (WS): Maintaining pattern and steeks, work to end.
Dec Row (RS): K1, ssk, pattern to last 3 sts, k2tog, k1. 2 sts dec'd
Work 1 row straight.
Repeat Dec Row. 2 sts dec'd
Repeat last 2 rows another 2 times. 157 (185: 183: 205: 231) sts; 25 (30: 31: 36: 41) sts each for Left and Right Front, 93 (111: 107: 119: 135) sts for Back and 7 sts per steek.

Natural and Traditional charts only

Work 9 rows straight, ending after a RS row. You should have completed Row 216 (243: 225: 243: 261) of Natural and Traditional charts.

Ombre charts only

Work 9 (9: 9: 8: 9) rows straight, ending after a RS (RS: RS: WS: RS) row. You should have completed Row 198 (225: 207: 224: 260) of Ombre charts.

All chart versions

You will now cast off steeks and work Back and Fronts separately.
Next row: Pattern 25 (30: 31: 36: 41) Front sts to steek, cast off next 7 steek sts, pattern until you have the 93 (111: 107: 119: 135) sts for Back on your right needle, cast off next 7 steek sts, pattern 25 (30: 31: 36: 41) Front sts to end, noting that the first of these sts will already be on your right needle after casting off.

Shape first front shoulder

Turn and continue on these last 25 (30: 31: 36: 41) Front sts only.
You will now work another 17 (8: 8: 8: 8) rows straight (all charts), but when you work these rows, work TOP DOWN through the previous rows of the chart before the row you worked when casting off the steeks. This means that the motif you've just worked will be mirrored and that the top edge of the front shoulder will join to the correct row of the pattern where it meets the back shoulder.
Work straight for set number of rows for your size as given above.
Leave on a stitch holder or spare needle. Break yarn.

Shape second front shoulder

Rejoin yarn with correct side facing for next row to 25 (30: 31: 36: 41) Front sts.

Work straight as for first shoulder for given number of rows for your size.

Interim finishing

With WS facing each other, and working from the armhole edge inwards, rejoin MC. Using Kitchener stitch, graft together the first 25 (30: 31: 36: 41) sts of Back together with the 25 (30: 31: 36: 41) sts of Left Shoulder, slip next 43 (51: 45: 47: 53) sts to waste yarn, leaving 25 (30: 31: 36: 41) sts on left needle. Using Kitchener stitch, graft together these sts with 25 (30: 31: 36: 41) sts of Right Shoulder.
Lay garment flat so that the shoulder joins are sitting at back, and place a waste yarn marker at left and right armhole edges of the new natural fold at the top of the shoulder.

WOMEN'S AND MEN'S VERSIONS

Sleeves

With MC and smaller double-pointed needles or short circular needles, cast on 56 (64: 64: 72: 80) sts.
Join to work in the round, being careful not to twist. Place marker for beginning of round.
Rib Round: *K2, p2; rep from * to end of round.
Work Rib Round another 6 (8: 6: 6: 8) times, increasing 1 st at end of last round. Rib should measure 2.5cm (1in) from cast-on edge. 57 (65: 65: 73: 81) sts.
Change to larger needles.

WOMEN'S VERSION ONLY

Begin with Row 37 of Natural and Traditional chart, or Row 19 (19: 19: 19: 37) of Ombre chart.

MEN'S VERSION ONLY

Begin with Row 19 of Natural and Traditional chart or Row 1 (1: 1: 1: 19) of Ombre chart.

WOMEN'S AND MEN'S VERSIONS

Starting your first row as given for your version and chart on st 21 (17: 17: 25: 21) of chart and ending with st 5 (9: 9: 1: 5) of chart, continue in colourwork pattern, noting that you will be working partial repeats of the pattern at beginning and end of rounds.
Work 11 (13: 13: 18: 19) rounds straight off chart as set.

Shape sleeve

Taking new sts into colourwork pattern, shape sleeves as follows.
Inc Round: K1, M1R, knit to last st, M1L, k1. 2 sts inc'd.
Work 7 (5: 5: 5: 3) rounds straight.
Repeat Inc Round once more. 2 sts inc'd.
Repeat last 8 (6: 6: 6: 4) rounds another 2 (2: 4: 11: 1) times. 65 (73: 77: 99: 87) sts
Work 9 (7: 7: 7: 5) rounds straight.
Repeat Inc Round once more. 2 sts inc'd
Repeat last 10 (8: 8: 8: 6) rounds another 7 (11: 8: 3: 17) times. 81 (97: 95: 107: 123) sts

Natural and Traditional charts only

Work straight until you have completed 144 (156: 144: 150: 163) rows of chart from beginning of colourwork. This will be row 162 (174: 162: 168: 181) of Natural and Traditional charts.

Ombre charts only

Work straight until you have completed 144 (156: 144: 150: 162) rows of chart from beginning of colourwork. This will be row 144 (156: 144: 150: 180) of Ombre charts.

Pattern continues overleaf

All chart versions

Shape top sleeve

You will now shape the top sleeve. To do this, you will need to work back and forth in rows, turning at edge each time. While shaping top sleeve, purl in pattern on WS rows and strand yarn not in use across WS of work.

Next row (RS): Cast off 2 sts, knit to marker, turn. 79 (95: 93: 105: 121) sts.
Next row (WS): Cast off 2 sts, purl to end. 77 (93: 91: 103: 119) sts.
Dec Row (RS): K1, ssk, k to last 3 sts, k2tog, k1. 2 sts dec'd.

Sizes S, M, L and XL only

Dec Row (WS): P1, p2tog, purl to last 3 sts, ssp, p1. 2 sts dec'd.
Dec Row (RS): K1, ssk, knit to last 3 sts, k2tog, k1. 2 sts dec'd.
Repeat last 2 rows another 0 (0: 0: 1: 1) times. 75 (87: 85: 93: 109) sts.

All sizes

Work 1 row straight.
Repeat RS Dec Row. 2 sts dec'd.
Repeat last 2 rows another 4 (6: 5: 10: 15) times. 65 (73: 73: 71: 77) sts.
Work 3 rows straight.
Repeat RS Dec Row. 2 sts dec'd.
Repeat last 4 rows another 4 (6: 5: 4: 6) times. 55 (59: 61: 61: 63) sts.

Natural and Traditional charts only

Work another 3 (8: 8: 5: 4) rows straight. You should have finished after row 198 (229: 211: 222: 252) of Natural and Traditional charts.

Ombre charts only

Work another 4 (5: 5: 5: 4) rows straight. You should have finished after row 181 (208: 190: 204: 251) of Ombre charts.

All chart versions

Leave sts on a holder. Work the second sleeve in the same way.

Finishing

Neck edging

WOMEN'S VERSION ONLY

With RS facing, using MC and smaller DPNs or short circular needles, and beginning at left shoulder seam, pick up and knit 7 (14: 14: 14: 14) sts up Left Back neck edge, pick up and knit 14 (21: 21: 21: 21) sts down Left Front neck edge, knit across 47 (55: 49: 55: 63) held Front neck sts, pick up and knit 14 (21: 21: 21: 21) sts up Right Front neck edge, pick up and knit 14 (21: 21: 21: 21) sts down Right Back neck edge, knit across 55 (63: 57: 63: 71) held Back neck sts. Pm for beg of round. 144 (188: 176: 188: 204) sts.

Rib Round: *K2, p2; rep from * to end of round.
Repeat Rib Round another 6 (8: 8: 8: 8) times.

MEN'S VERSION ONLY

With RS facing, using MC and smaller DPNs or short circular needles, and beginning at left shoulder seam, pick up and knit 7 sts up Left Back neck edge, pick up and knit 14 sts down Left Front neck edge, knit across 35 (43: 37: 39: 45) held Front neck sts, pick up and knit 14 sts up Right Front neck edge, pick up and knit 7 sts down Right Back neck edge, knit across 43 (51: 45: 47: 53) held Back neck sts. Pm for beg of round. 120 (136: 124: 128: 140) sts.
Rib Round: *K2, p2; rep from * to end of round.
Repeat Rib Round another 7 (8: 8: 8: 8) times.

WOMEN'S AND MEN'S VERSIONS

Cast off in rib, ensuring cast-offs opposite shoulder seams and across back neck are worked relatively firmly, to avoid the rib edging flaring out.

Underarm finishing

Crochet 2 chains up each steek, 1 st either side of the central stitch.
Carefully cut open each steek with a pair of small sharp scissors, by cutting through the central stitch. Fold back, using the purl stitch as a guide, and catch down the edges to the inside of the garment.

Attach sleeves

Set in sleeves, lining up centre of top sleeve with marker at top shoulder edge.
Place a marker in waste yarn at centre of shoulder.
With a smaller circular needle, pick up but do not knit 27 (29: 30: 30: 31) sts across top edge of first side of armhole, pick up but do not knit 1 st at centre of shoulder in line with waste yarn marker, pick up but do not knit 27 (29: 30: 30: 31) sts across top edge of second side of armhole. 55 (59: 61: 61: 63) sts
Slip sleeve sts onto a spare needle and line up centre of top sleeve sts with waste yarn marker.
Using Kitchener stitch, graft sleeve into armhole, leaving side shaping of armhole and sleeve, and underarm and sleeve top cast offs ungrafted.
Join underarm and sleeve shapings and cast offs together using false grafting.
Weave in ends and block to measurements given at the beginning of the pattern.

Ombre colourway
Extra Small

☐	Knit
☐	Pattern repeat
■	727 Admiral Navy
■	168 Clyde Blue
■	136 Teviot
■	134 Blue Danube
■	106 Mooskit
■	105 Eesit
■	478 Amber
■	578 Rust

COLOUR CODE	NO. 25G BALLS NEEDED XS
727 >	3
168 >	3
136 >	3
134 >	3
106 >	5
105 >	3
478 >	1
578 >	1

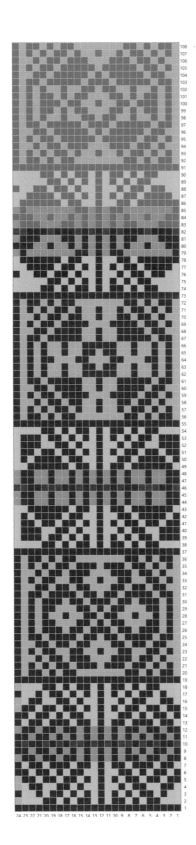

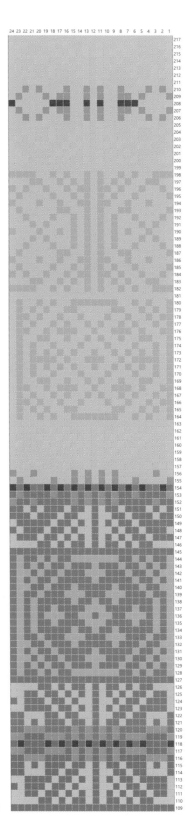

CREW NECK JUMPER

Ombre colourway
Small / Medium

88

	Knit
	Pattern repeat
■	727 Admiral Navy
■	168 Clyde Blue
■	136 Teviot
■	134 Blue Danube
■	106 Mooskit
■	105 Eesit
■	478 Amber
■	578 Rust

COLOUR CODE	NO. 25G BALLS NEEDED	
	S	M
727 >	4	4
168 >	3	3
136 >	3	3
134 >	4	4
106 >	5	6
105 >	4	4
478 >	1	1
578 >	1	1

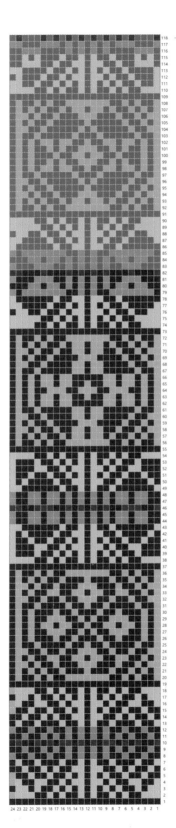

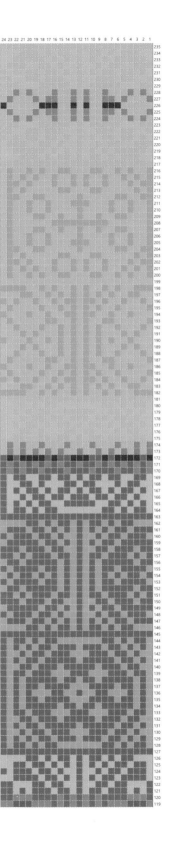

Ombre colourway
Large / Extra Large

☐	Knit	
☐	Pattern repeat	
■	727 Admiral Navy	
■	168 Clyde Blue	
■	136 Teviot	
■	134 Blue Danube	
■	106 Mooskit	
■	105 Eesit	
■	478 Amber	
■	578 Rust	

NO. 25G BALLS NEEDED

COLOUR CODE	L	XL		L	XL		L	XL		L	XL
727 >	4	4	136 >	3	3	106 >	6	6	478 >	1	1
168 >	3	3	134 >	4	4	105 >	4	4	578 >	1	1

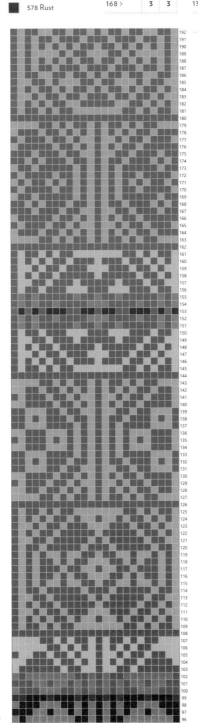

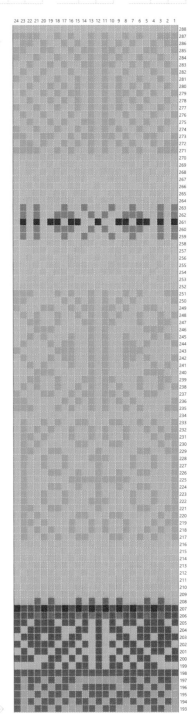

89

SLASH NECK JUMPER

This jumper was inspired by the garments knitted on Fair Isle during the 19th century. It is quick to knit as it doesn't require shaping, keeping all the focus on the colourwork. In the 19th century, this type of garment was probably knitted for daily use and possibly knitted by children, too.

YARN

Jamieson's of Shetland,
Shetland Spindrift
4ply weight,
100% Shetland wool,
105m (115yd) per 25g ball

Natural colourway

● 101 Natural Black **MC**

○ 104 Natural White

Traditional colourway

● 101 Natural Black **MC**

● 587 Madder

● 289 Gold

● 726 Prussian

○ 104 Natural White

Ombre colourway

● 727 Admiral Navy

○ 105 Eesit

● 478 Amber

● 578 Rust

○ 106 Mooskit

● 168 Clyde Blue

● 136 Teviot

○ 134 Blue Danube

For number of balls of yarn required for each size, refer to colourway charts.

SIZE	XS	S	M	L	XL
To fit chest circumference (approx)	81–86cm 32–34in	91–97cm 36–38in	102–107cm 40–42in	112–117cm 44–46in	122–127cm 48–50in
Actual chest circumference	96cm 37¾in	107cm 42in	112cm 44in	124.5cm 49in	137cm 54in
Length to side shoulder	57.5cm 22½in	58.5cm 23in	62.5cm 24¾in	64.5cm 25½in	71.5cm 28¼in
Armhole depth	20cm 7¾in	22cm 8½in	24cm 9½in	24.5cm 9¾in	30cm 11¾in
Back neck width	25cm 9¾in	26.5cm 10¼in	26.5cm 10¼in	27cm 10½in	27.5cm 10¾in
Sleeve length	50cm 19¾in	51cm 20in	55cm 21¾in	56cm 22in	53cm 21in
Cuff circumference	20.5cm 8in	21cm 8¼in	22.5cm 8¾in	23.5cm 9¼in	24.5cm 9¾in
Top sleeve circumference	42cm 16½in	45.5cm 18in	51cm 20in	52cm 20½in	64cm 25¼in

Above: Jumper knitted by Rebecca Snelling LeRoy
Opposite: Feeding sheep at Taft Croft
Jumper knitted by Elbia Sylwestrzak

TENSION

All the garments in this book have been created using different tensions depending on the size being knitted. This allows us to offer a variety of sizes without having to use partial repeats of the 24-stitch patterns.

You may need to experiment with needle sizes to achieve the required tension for your size. If you've achieved the correct stitch tension but your round/row tension is wrong, try changing needle size by the smallest increment available, as this will often be enough to alter your round/row tension without compromising your stitch tension.

If you find you can only achieve stitch tension but not round/row tension, remember that you can still block out a small difference in round/row tension. Always block your swatch in the same way that you will block the finished garment. See page 141 for blocking instructions.

Sizes XS and M only

30 stitches and 34 rounds (rows) to 10cm (4in), measured over blocked stranded colourwork, using 2.75mm (US 2, UK 12) needles.

If necessary, change your needle size to achieve the stated tension.

Sizes S and L only

27 stitches and 30 rounds (rows) to 10cm (4in), measured over blocked stranded colourwork, using 3.25mm (US 3, UK 10) needles.

If necessary, change your needle size to achieve the stated tension.

Size XL only

28 stitches and 32 rounds (rows) to 10cm (4in), measured over blocked stranded colourwork, using 3mm (US 2/3, UK 11) needles.

If necessary, change your needle size to achieve the stated tension.

NEEDLES & NOTIONS

Circular needle two sizes below the size for the stated tension, 80cm (32in) long
Circular needle two sizes below the size for the stated gauge, 40cm (16in) or 60cm (24in) long
Circular needle for the stated tension, 80cm (32in) long

1 set double-pointed needles for the stated tension
1 set double-pointed needles, two sizes below the size for the stated gauge

1 stitch marker plus 11 (11: 13: 13: 15) stitch markers, in a contrasting colour (optional)

Tapestry needle
Small crochet hook
Needle and polyester or wool thread
Small sharp scissors

NOTES

When working colourwork sections, strand colour not in use evenly across the back (wrong side) of your work.

All chart rows should be read from right to left when working in the round.

When working flat in rows, read RS rows from right to left and WS rows from left to right.

Armholes are made by casting off body stitches and then casting on for steeks, which are cut open later and stitched down.

INSTRUCTIONS

With MC and smaller, 80cm (32in) long circular needles, make a slip knot and place on needle as the first st, leaving a long tail for casting on; cast on 1 st using the long-tail cast-on method, then cast on 2 sts using the twisted German cast-on method. *Cast on 2 sts using the long-tail cast-on method, cast on 2 sts using the twisted German cast-on method; repeat from * until there are 288 (288: 336: 336: 384) sts on the needle. Join to work in the round, being careful not to twist. Place marker for beginning of round.

Pattern continues overleaf

Natural colourway

Knit

Pattern repeat

■ 101 Natural Black

□ 104 Natural White

COLOUR CODE	NO. 25G BALLS NEEDED				
	XS	S	M	L	XL
101 >	11	12	13	15	17
104 >	9	10	12	13	15

93

Follow written pattern below and refer to chart for colourwork placement only.

Hem

Rib Round: *K2, p2; rep from * to end of round.

Work Rib Round another 13 (11: 13: 11: 11) times.

Body

Change to larger circular needles.

Work colourwork section, repeating the 24-stitch pattern 12 (12: 14: 14: 16) times per round and placing markers after each repeat, if desired, on first of these rounds.

Continue in colourwork pattern until you have completed Row 112 (98: 118: 108: 120) of chart, ending last round 3 (3: 5: 5: 5) sts before end of round.

Shape armholes and set steeks

Next Round: Cast off 7 (7: 9: 9: 9) sts, pattern until you have 137 (137: 159: 159: 183) sts on your needles, cast off the next 7 (7: 9: 9: 9) sts, pattern 137 (137: 159: 159: 183) sts to end of round, noting that the first of these sts will already be on your right needle after casting off. DO NOT BREAK YARN.

You will now cast on for steeks across both armholes.

Next Round: Using the backwards loop method and MC of current round, cast on 7 sts across left underarm cast-off, pattern across 137 (137: 159: 159: 183) sts for Front, cast on 7 sts across right underarm cast-off, pattern across 137 (137: 159: 159: 183) sts for Back. 288 (288: 332: 332: 380) sts total; 137 (137: 159: 159: 183) sts each for Front and Back and 7 sts for each steek.

When working steek stitches, use two colours, alternating every other stitch to create a chequerboard or stripe effect.

Steeks should always be worked as follows: P1, k5, p1, with MC of round worked for the first and last stitches. If you are changing colours, do so in the middle of the steek.

Purling at the edges of the steek allows you to fold back the edge easily later.

Continue working straight, keeping Front and Back pattern and steeks correct until you have completed Row 180 (162: 198: 180: 216) of chart.

Next Round: Cast off 7 sts for steek, pattern across 137 (137: 159: 159: 183) sts for Front, cast off 7 sts for steek, pattern across 137 (137: 159: 159: 183) sts for Back. 274 (274: 318: 318: 366) sts total; 137 (137: 159: 159: 183) sts each for Front and Back. Break yarns.

Interim finishing

With WS facing each other and working from the armhole edge inwards, rejoin MC. Using Kitchener stitch, graft together the 31 (33: 40: 43: 53) Front and Back shoulder sts.

Again working from the armhole edge inwards, do the same at the other shoulder. The centre 75 (71: 79: 73: 77) sts on Front and Back remain unworked.

Turn garment right side out.

Neck edging

Change to smaller DPNs or short circular needles. With MC, beginning at left shoulder seam, knit 150 (142: 158: 146: 154) sts around neck edge.

This edging is worked by using two separate strands of the same colour, alternating them across each round. In this way, you create a single-colour form of stranded colourwork, which will prevent the top edge from rolling over too much while remaining at the same tension as the colourwork section you have already worked.

For the second strand, pull from the centre of the ball.

If you are following the chart, you will see a symbol indicating when to use the second strand, given here as kwss.

Round 1: *K1, kwss; rep from * to end of round.

Round 2: *Kwss, k1; rep from * to end of round.

Pattern continues overleaf

Traditional colourway

	Knit
	Pattern repeat
■	101 Natural Black
▨	289 Gold
▨	587 Madder
■	726 Prussian
☐	104 Natural White

COLOUR CODE	NO. 25G BALLS NEEDED				
	XS	S	M	L	XL
101 >	4	5	5	6	6
298 >	4	4	4	5	5
587 >	4	5	5	6	6
726 >	4	5	5	6	6
104 >	7	7	8	9	10

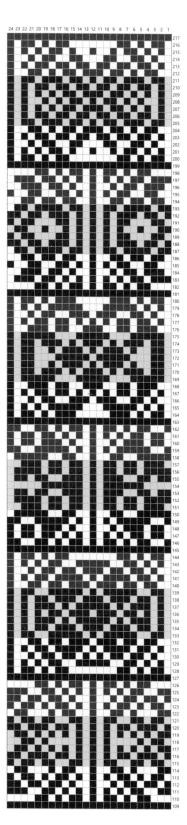

95

Work 5 more rounds as set. Cut second strand of MC.

Work in st st for 3 rounds.

Cast off loosely but neatly.

Set aside while you work the sleeves.

Sleeves

With MC and smaller DPNs, cast on 61 (57: 67: 63: 69) sts.

Join to work in the round, being careful not to twist.
Place marker for beginning of round.

Knit 2 rounds.

Round 1: *K1, kwss; rep from * to last st, k1.

Round 2: *Kwss, k1; rep from * to last st, kwss.

Repeat Rounds 1–2 once more.

Change to larger DPNs.

Beginning with st 19 (21: 16: 18: 15) of chart and row 1 and ending with st 7 (5: 10: 8: 11), continue in colourwork pattern, noting that you will need to work partial repeats of the pattern at beginning and end of rounds, and working a total of 18 (16: 18: 16: 16) rows of chart as set.

Shape sleeve

Taking new sts into colourwork pattern, shape sleeves as follows.

Inc Round: K1, M1R, k to last st, M1L, k1. 2 sts inc'd.

Work 3 (1: 1: 1: 1) rounds straight.

Repeat Inc Round once more. 2 sts inc'd.

Repeat last 4 (2: 2: 2: 2) rounds another 28 (4: 9: 9: 41) times. 121 (69: 89: 85: 155) sts.

Work 5 (3: 3: 3: 3) rounds straight.

Repeat Inc Round once more. 2 sts inc'd.

Repeat last 6 (4: 4: 4: 4) rounds another 2 (26: 31: 27: 11) times. 127 (123: 153: 141: 179) sts.

Work another 5 (6: 6: 7: 7) rounds straight, ending last round 3 (3: 5: 5: 5) sts before end of round. Cast off next 6 (6: 10: 10: 10) sts. 121 (117: 143: 131: 169) sts.

Leave sts on a holder.

Repeat pattern for second sleeve.

Finishing

Underarm finishing

Crochet 2 chains up the steek, 1 st either side of the central stitch.

Carefully cut open steek with a pair of small sharp scissors, by cutting through the central stitch. Fold back, using the purl stitch as a guide, and catch down the edges to the inside of the garment.

Place a marker in waste yarn at centre of shoulder.

With a smaller circular needle, pick up but do not knit 60 (58: 71: 65: 84) sts up first side of armhole, pick up but do not knit 1 st at centre of shoulder in line with waste yarn marker, pick up but do not knit 60 (58: 71: 65: 84) sts down second side of armhole. 121 (117: 143: 131: 169) sts.

Line up centre of top sleeve with waste yarn marker.

Using Kitchener stitch, graft sleeve into armhole, leaving underarm and sleeve top cast offs ungrafted.

Join underarm and sleeve top cast offs together using false grafting.

Repeat for second sleeve.

Weave in ends and block to measurements given at the beginning of the pattern.

Ombre colourway
Extra Small / Small / Large

☐	Knit
☐	Pattern repeat
■	727 Admiral Navy
■	105 Eesit
■	106 Mooskit
■	478 Amber
■	578 Rust
■	168 Clyde Blue
■	136 Teviot
■	134 Blue Danube

COLOUR CODE	NO. 25G BALLS NEEDED		
	XS	S	M
727 >	3	3	4
105 >	5	5	6
106 >	4	5	5
487 >	2	2	2
578 >	1	1	1
168 >	3	3	3
136 >	4	5	5
134 >	4	5	5

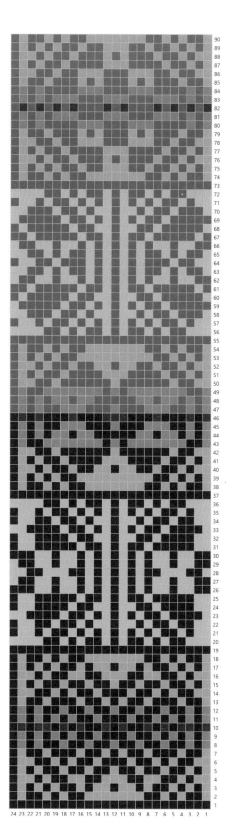

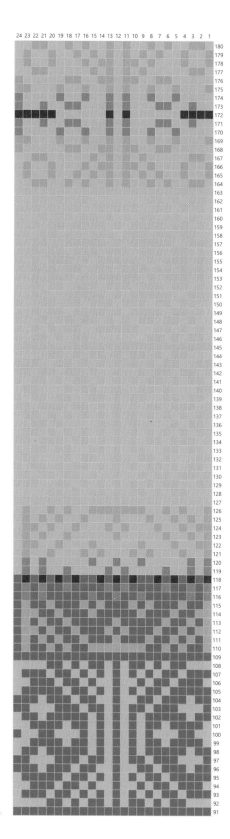

97

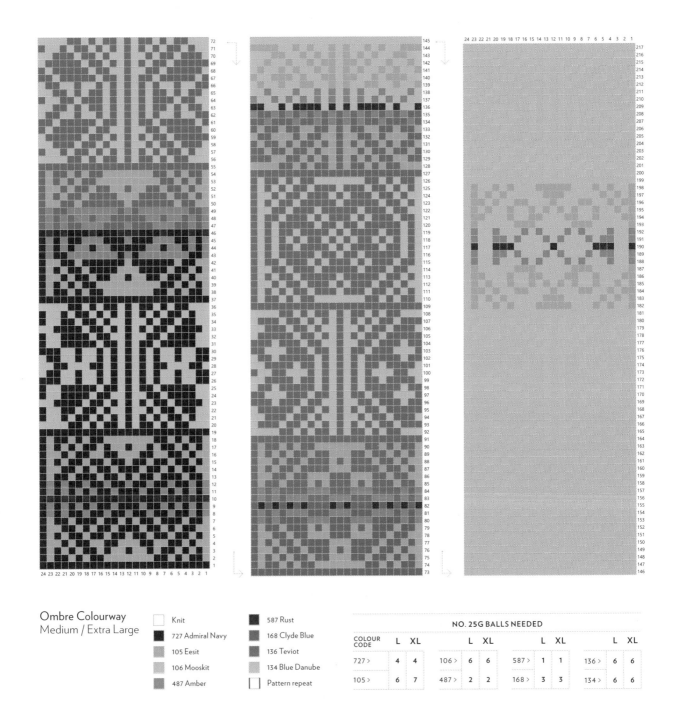

Ombre Colourway
Medium / Extra Large

	Knit
■	727 Admiral Navy
■	105 Eesit
■	106 Mooskit
■	487 Amber

■	587 Rust
■	168 Clyde Blue
■	136 Teviot
	134 Blue Danube
☐	Pattern repeat

NO. 25G BALLS NEEDED

COLOUR CODE	L	XL		L	XL		L	XL		L	XL
727 >	4	4	106 >	6	6	587 >	1	1	136 >	6	6
105 >	6	7	487 >	2	2	168 >	3	3	134 >	6	6

Opposite: Chapel at Taft croft

PAST AND PRESENT

Early pieces of Fair Isle knitting use four colours: two foreground colours and two background colours with a combination of 'muckle and eleven geeng flooers' (large and medium size motifs). Most of the garments of the 1904 Bruce Antarctic Expedition were knitted in this fashion as well as several museum pieces, including the garment portrayed in Stanley Cursiters' 1923 painting, The Fair Isle Jumper.

In this group of projects I use what I call the 'two by two' formula to explore the use of colour, progressing into 6 colours, while also examining the use of 'highlights' within the motif, a method developed by the knitters in mainland Shetland.

101

View of SheepRock from North Haven

HAND WARMERS

These hand warmers are a cross between wrist warmers and fingerless gloves. This pattern is very easy, as it only requires a thumb opening and doesn't use a rib effect. It is quick to knit and a good way to practise colourwork or test new colourways.

SIZE	S / M
To fit hand circumference measured around knuckles	15–22cm 6–8½in
Finished circumference	18cm 7in
Finished height	24cm 9½in

YARN

Jamieson's of Shetland, Shetland Spindrift
4ply weight, 100% Shetland wool, 105m (115yd) per 25g ball

Natural colourway
- ● **1** × 101 Natural Black **MC**
- ○ **1** × 104 Natural White

Traditional colourway
- ● **1** × 101 Natural Black **MC**
- ● **1** × 289 Gold
- ● **1** × 587 Madder
- ● **1** × 726 Prussian
- ○ **1** × 104 Natural White

Striped colourway
- ● **1** × 825 Olive
- ● **1** × 101 Natural Black
- ● **1** × 102 Shaela
- ● **1** × 106 Mooskit
- ○ **1** × 104 Natural White
- ● **1** × 578 Rust

TENSION

27 stitches and 30 rounds to 10cm (4in), measured over blocked, stranded colourwork, using 3.25mm (US 3, UK 10) needles.

If necessary, change your needle size to achieve the stated tension.

NEEDLES & NOTIONS

1 set 3.25mm (US 3, UK 10) double-pointed needles or long circular needle if using magic loop method

Tapestry needle

1 stitch marker

NOTES

When working colourwork sections, strand colour not in use evenly across the back (wrong side) of your work.

All chart rounds should be read from right to left, apart from Rows 20–39, which are worked back and forth in rows, starting with a RS (knit) row.

INSTRUCTIONS

With MC, cast on 48 sts using the long-tail or twisted German cast-on method.

Join to work in the round, being careful not to twist. Place marker for beginning of round.

Hand warmers can be worked entirely from chart, repeating the 48-stitch pattern once per round.

If this is your preferred method, read the section below on Lower Edging before working Rounds 2–3. Follow chart until you have completed Round 71, then cast off purlwise.

Alternatively, follow written pattern below and refer to chart for colourwork section only.

Lower edging

Round 1: Knit to end of round.

This edging is worked by using two separate strands of the same colour, alternating them across each round. In this way, you create a single-colour form of stranded colourwork, which will prevent the top edge of the hand warmers from rolling over while remaining at the same tension as the colourwork section you will work next.

For the second strand, pull from the centre of the ball.

If you are following the chart, you will see a symbol indicating when to use the second strand, given here as kwss.

Round 2: *K1, kwss; rep from * to end of round.

Round 3: *Kwss, k1; rep from * to end of round.

Cut second strand of MC.

Main section

Rounds 4–38: Knit, following chart.

Row 39 (RS): Knit, following chart, to last 2 sts, ssk using colour shown on chart. Turn. 47 sts.

Rows 40–53: Beginning with a WS (purl) row, continue working back and forth in rows, stranding colour not in use across WS of work.

Round 54: Knit to end, cast on 1 st over gap using backward loop method and pulling tightly to avoid making a loose stitch. Do not turn, continue knitting in the round. 48 sts.

Rounds 55–68: Knit, following chart.

Upper edging

Round 69: Using colour shown on chart, *kwss, k1; rep from * to end of round.

Round 70: *K1, kwss; rep from * to end of round.
Round 71: Knit to end of round.

Cast off purlwise. Repeat pattern for second hand warmer.

Finishing

Weave in ends and block to measurements given at the beginning of the pattern.

104

Natural colourway

- ☐ Knit on RS / Purl on WS
- ◇ Kwss
- ＼ SSK
- ◡ Cast on
- ☐ Work in rows
- ☐ Centre stitch
- ■ 101 Natural Black
- ☐ 104 Natural White

Traditional colourway

Knit on RS / Purl on WS
◇ Kwss
╲ SSK
◡ Cast on
▢ Work in rows
▢ Centre stitch
■ 101 Natural Black
▨ 289 Gold
▨ 587 Madder
▨ 726 Prussian
□ 104 Nautral White

Striped colourway

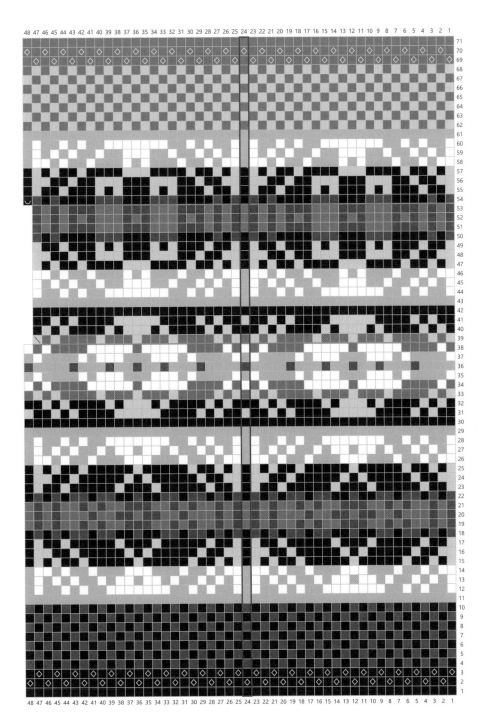

☐	Knit on RS / Purl on WS
◇	Kwss
╲	SSK
⌣	Cast on
☐	Work in rows
☐	Centre stitch
■	825 Olive
■	101 Natural Black
■	102 Shaela
■	106 Mooskit
☐	104 Natural White
■	578 Rust

NECK WARMER

The neck warmer was designed with mountain sports in mind as it is practical, small, lightweight, and warm. It is easy to knit and a good step up if you are a beginner knitter and feel confident with colourwork.

SIZE	S/M	M/L
Finished circumference	53cm	62cm
	21in	24½in
Finished height	22cm	
	8½in	

YARN

Jamieson's of Shetland, Shetland Spindrift
4ply weight, 100% Shetland wool, 105m (115yd) per 25g ball

Natural colourway

● **2 ×** 101 Natural Black **MC**

○ **1 ×** 104 Natural White

Traditional colourway

● **2 ×** 101 Natural Black **MC**

● **1 ×** 289 Gold

● **1 ×** 587 Madder

● **1 ×** 726 Prussian

○ **1 ×** 104 Natural White

Striped colourway

● **2 ×** 825 Olive

● **1 ×** 101 Natural Black

● **1 ×** 102 Shaela

○ **1 ×** 106 Mooskit

○ **1 ×** 104 Natural White

● **1 ×** 578 Rust

Above: Neck warmer knitted by Margaret Milligan
Opposite: Tractor at the quarry
Neck warmer knitted by Anita Barlett

TENSION

27 stitches and 30 rounds to 10cm (4in), measured over blocked stranded colourwork, using 3.25mm (US 3, UK 10) needles.

If necessary, change your needle size to achieve the stated tension.

NEEDLES & NOTIONS

2.75mm (US 2, UK 12) circular needle, 40cm (16in) long

3.25mm (US 3, UK 10) circular needle, 40cm (16in) long

Tapestry needle

1 stitch marker plus 5 (6) stitch markers, in a contrasting colour (optional)

NOTES

When working colourwork sections, strand colour not in use evenly across the back (wrong side) of your work.

Read all chart rounds from right to left.

INSTRUCTIONS

With MC and smaller needles, make a slip knot and place on needle as the first st, leaving a long tail for casting on. Cast on 1 st using the long-tail cast-on method, then cast on 2 sts using the twisted German cast-on method. *Cast on 2 sts using the long-tail cast-on method, cast on 2 sts using the twisted German cast-on method; repeat from * until there are 144 (168) sts on the needle.

Join to work in the round, being careful not to twist. Place marker for beginning of round.

Neck warmer can be worked entirely from chart, repeating the 24-stitch pattern 6 (7) times per round and placing markers every 24 sts to denote repeats, if desired, on Round 13.

If this is your preferred method, follow chart, changing to larger needles when rib is complete, until you have completed Round 57. Read section below on Upper Edging before working Rounds 58–66.

When Round 67 is complete cast off purlwise.

Alternatively, follow written pattern below and refer to chart for colourwork section only.

Lower edging

Rib Round: *K2, p2; rep from * to end of round.

Work Rib Round another 11 times.

Main section

Change to larger needles.

Work colourwork section, following Rounds 13–57 of chart, repeating the 24-stitch pattern 6 (7) times per round and placing markers every 24 sts to denote repeats, if desired, on first of these rounds.

Upper edging

This edging is worked by using two separate strands of the same colour, alternating them across each round. In this way, you create a single-colour form of stranded colourwork, which will prevent the top edge of the neck warmer from rolling over while remaining at the same tension as the colourwork section you have just worked.

For the second strand, pull from the centre of the ball.

If you are following the chart, you will see a symbol indicating when to use the second strand, given here as kwss.

Upper Edging Round: *K1, kwss; rep from * to end of round.

Work Upper Edging Round another 8 times.

Round 67: Knit to end of round.

Cast off purlwise.

Finishing

Weave in ends and block to measurements given at the beginning of the pattern.

Natural
colourway

Traditional
colourway

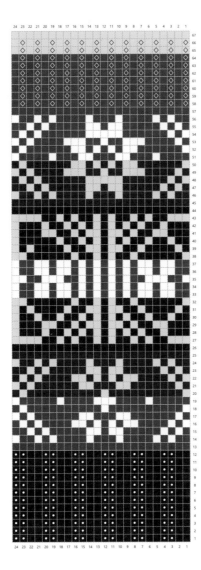

Striped
colourway

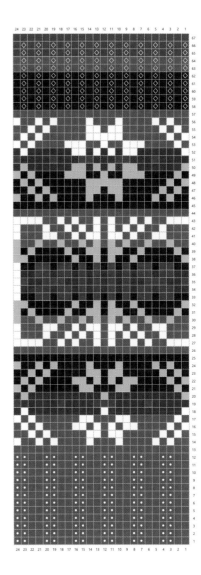

	Knit on RS
•	Purl
◇	Kwss
■	101 Natural Black
□	104 Natural White

	Knit
•	Purl
◇	Kwss
■	101 Natural Black
■	289 Gold
■	587 Madder
■	726 Prussian
□	104 Nautral White

	Knit
•	Purl
◇	Kwss
■	825 Olive
■	101 Natural Black
■	102 Shaela
■	106 Mooskit
□	104 Natural White
■	578 Rust

SKI HAT

This design is based on the hats produced for après-skiing, with a folded rib to add extra warmth around the ears and a pompom or tassel in a contrasting colour. The motif arrangement is one of the most traditional ones, with the Fivey Flooers and the Muckle Flooers creating 'bands' within the design in addition to the background bands of colour.

SIZE		S	M	L
To fit head circumference (approx)		44cm 17¼in	52cm 20½in	60cm 23½in
Actual hat circumference at brim		40cm 15¾in	48cm 19in	56cm 22in
Ski Hat length	Brim unfolded	28cm 11in	Brim folded	22.5cm 8¾in

YARN

Jamieson's of Shetland, Shetland Spindrift
4ply weight, 100% Shetland wool, 105m (115yd) per 25g ball

Natural colourway
- **2 ×** 101 Natural Black **MC**
- **1 ×** 104 Natural White

Traditional colourway
- **2 ×** 101 Natural Black **MC**
- **1 ×** 289 Gold
- **1 ×** 587 Madder
- **1 ×** 726 Prussian
- **1 ×** 104 Natural White

Striped colourway
- **2 ×** 825 Olive
- **1 ×** 101 Natural Black
- **1 ×** 102 Shaela
- **1 ×** 106 Mooskit
- **1 ×** 104 Natural White
- **1 ×** 578 Rust

Above: Hat knitted by Margaret Milligan
Opposite: Feeding sheep at Taft Croft
Hat knitted by Judith Sogan

TENSION

30 stitches and 34 rounds/ rows to 10cm (4in), measured over blocked stranded colourwork, using 2.75mm (US 2, UK 12) needles

If necessary, change your needle size to achieve the stated tension.

NEEDLES & NOTIONS

1 set 2.25mm (US 1, UK 13) double-pointed needles or long circular needle for magic loop method

1 set 2.75mm (US 2, UK 12) double-pointed needles or long circular needle for magic loop method

1 stitch marker plus 4 (5: 6) stitch markers, in a contrasting colour (optional)

Tapestry needle

Pompom-making tools

NOTE

When working colourwork sections, strand colour not in use evenly across the back (wrong side) of your work.

All chart rows should be read from right to left.

INSTRUCTIONS

With MC and smaller needles, make a slip knot and place on needle as the first st, leaving a long tail for casting on. Cast on 1 st using the long-tail cast-on method, then cast on 2 sts using the twisted German cast-on method. *Cast on 2 sts using the long-tail cast-on method, cast on 2 sts using the twisted German cast-on method; repeat from * until there are 120 (144: 168) sts on the needle. Join to work in the round, being careful not to twist. Place marker for beginning of round.

Hat can be worked entirely from chart, repeating the 24-stitch pattern 5 (6: 7) times per round. If this is your preferred method, follow chart to end, changing to larger needles when rib is complete, and then follow Round 97 as written below – this round is not shown on chart.

Alternatively, follow written pattern below and refer to chart for colourwork section only.

Brim

Rib Round: *K2, p2; rep from * to end of round.

Work Rib Round another 18 times.

Round 20 (fold): Purl to end of round.

Alt Rib Round: *P2, k2; rep from * to end of round.

Work Alt Rib Round another 17 times.

Main section

Change to larger needles.

Work colourwork section, following Rows 39–83 of chart, repeating the 24-stitch pattern 5 (6: 7) times per round, and placing markers every 24 sts to denote repeats, if desired, on first of these rounds.

Colourwork section is now complete.

Round 84: With colour indicated on chart for your colourway, knit to end of round, removing any pattern repeat markers as you come to them.

Crown decreases

Round 85: *K6, k2tog; rep from * to end of round. 15 (18: 21) sts dec'd. 105 (126: 147) sts.

Round 86: Knit to end of round.

Round 87: *K5, k2tog; rep from * to end of round. 15 (18: 21) sts dec'd. 90 (108: 126) sts.

Round 88: Knit to end of round.

Pattern continues overleaf

Round 89: *K4, k2tog; rep from * to end of round. 15 (18: 21) sts dec'd. 75 (90: 105) sts.

Round 90: Knit to end of round.

Round 91: *K3, k2tog; rep from * to end of round. 15 (18: 21) sts dec'd. 60 (72: 84) sts.

Round 92: Knit to end of round.

Round 93: *K2, k2tog; rep from * to end of round. 15 (18: 21) sts dec'd. 45 (54: 63) sts.

Round 94: Knit to end of round.

Round 95: *K1, k2tog; rep from * to end of round. 15 (18: 21) sts dec'd. 30 (36: 42) sts.

Round 96: *K2tog; rep from * to end of round. 15 (18: 21) sts dec'd. 15 (18: 21) sts.

Round 97 (not shown on chart): K1 (0: 1), *k2tog; rep from * to end of round. 7 (9: 10) sts dec'd. 8 (9: 11) sts.

Finishing

Break yarn and thread through remaining sts. Pull firmly to fasten, being careful not to break yarn.

Weave in ends and block to measurements given at the beginning of the pattern.

Fold brim back at Round 14 and catch in place if desired with whip stitches.

Pompom

Using one contrasting colour, make a medium-size pompom. Use a double strand of yarn to secure the centre, leaving enough length to secure to the crown. Trim the pompom to shape, and secure to the crown with the extra length of yarn. Weave in the ends on the inside around the closed stitches.

Alternatively, you can add a tassel to your hat, as shown on page 113 (see page 30 for instructions).

Natural colourway

☐ Knit
• Purl
╱ K2tog
■ 101 Natural Black
☐ 104 Natural White

Traditional colourway

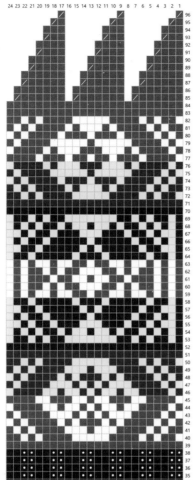

Knit

• Purl

⟋ K2tog

■ 101 Natural Black

☐ 289 Gold

■ 587 Madder

■ 726 Prussian

☐ 104 Natural White

Striped colourway

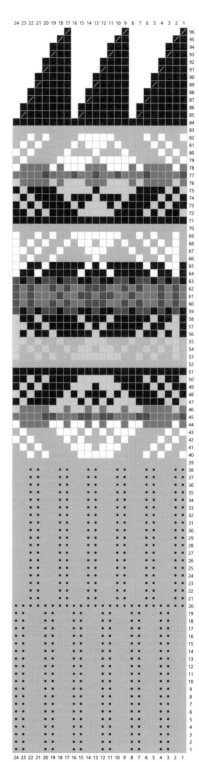

Knit

• Purl

⟋ K2tog

■ 825 Olive

■ 101 Natural Black

■ 102 Shaela

☐ 106 Mooskit

☐ 104 Natural White

■ 578 Rust

117

FISHERMAN'S JUMPER

This fisherman's jumper is the most traditional garment in this book, and more complex in construction, so it is a project for the experienced knitter. The design is an adaptation of the original garments knitted in the 19th century. The underarm gusset has been replaced by shaping the armhole and the sleeve, the neck has been shaped both in the back and the front, and the shoulder fasteners have been preserved.

YARN

Jamieson's of Shetland, Shetland Spindrift 4ply weight, 100% Shetland wool, 105m (115yd) per 25g ball

Natural colourway
- 101 Natural Black **MC**
- 104 Natural White

Traditional colourway
- 101 Natural Black **MC**
- 289 Gold
- 587 Madder
- 726 Prussian
- 104 Natural White

Striped colourway
- 825 Olive
- 101 Natural Black
- 102 Shaela
- 106 Mooskit
- 104 Natural White
- 578 Rust

For number of balls of yarn required for each size, refer to colourway charts

SIZE	XS	S	M	L	XL
To fit chest circumference (approx)	81–86cm 32–34in	91–97cm 36–38in	102–107cm 40–42in	112–117cm 44–46in	122–127cm 48–50in
Actual chest circumference	96cm 37¾in	107cm 42in	112cm 44in	124.5cm 49in	137cm 54in
Length to side shoulder as worn	58cm 22¾in	62cm 24½in	64.5cm 25½in	62cm 24½in	68.5cm 27in
Armhole depth as worn	19cm 7½in	22cm 8½in	25cm 9¾in	26cm 10¼in	29cm 11½in
Back neck width	17.5cm 7in	18.5cm 7¼in	19.5cm 7½in	20cm 7¾in	20.5cm 8in
Front neck depth, measured from side neck shoulder as worn	7.5cm 3in	7.5cm 3in	7.5cm 3in	7.5cm 3in	7.5cm 3in
Sleeve length	45cm 17¾in	51cm 20in	49cm 19¼in	51cm 20in	52cm 20½in
Cuff circumference	20.5cm 8in	22cm 8½in	23cm 9in	25cm 9¾in	26cm 10¼in
Top sleeve circumference	41.5cm 16½in	47.5cm 18¾in	54cm 21¼in	56.5cm 22¼in	61.5cm 24¼in

Above: Jumper knitted by Kristel Vervoort
Opposite: Lobster catching at North Haven
Jumper knitted by Diana Sutton

TENSION

All the garments in this book have been created using different tensions depending on the size being knitted. This allows us to offer a variety of sizes without having to use partial repeats of the 24-stitch patterns.

You may need to experiment with needle sizes to achieve the required tension for your size. If you've achieved the correct stitch tension but your round/row tension is wrong, try changing needle size by the smallest increment available, as this will often be enough to alter your round/row tension without compromising your stitch tension.

If you find you can only achieve stitch tension but not round/row tension, remember that you can still block out a small difference in round/row tension. Always block your swatch in the same way that you will block the finished garment. See page 141 for blocking instructions.

Sizes XS and M only

30 stitches and 34 rounds (rows) to 10cm (4in), measured over blocked stranded colourwork, using 2.75mm (US 2, UK 12) needles.

If necessary, change your needle size to achieve the stated tension.

Sizes S and L only

27 stitches and 30 rounds (rows) to 10cm (4in), measured over blocked stranded colourwork, using 3.25mm (US 3, UK 10) needles.

If necessary, change your needle size to achieve the stated tension.

Size XL only

28 stitches and 32 rounds (rows) to 10cm (4in), measured over blocked stranded colourwork, using 3mm (US 2/3, UK 11) needles.

If necessary, change your needle size to achieve the stated tension.

NEEDLES & NOTIONS

Circular needle two sizes below the size for the stated tension, 80cm (32in) long

Circular needle for the stated tension, 80cm (32in) long

1 set double-pointed needles for the stated tension

1 set double-pointed needles or shorter circular needle two sizes below the size for the stated tension

1 stitch marker plus 11 (11: 13: 13: 15) stitch markers, in a contrasting colour (optional)

5 x 2cm (³/₄in) buttons
Tapestry needle
Small crochet hook
Needle and polyester or wool thread
Small sharp scissors

NOTES

When working colourwork sections, strand colour not in use evenly across the back (wrong side) of your work.

All chart rows should be read from right to left when working in the round.

When working flat in rows, read odd-numbered rows from right to left and even-numbered rows from left to right.

Armholes are made by casting off body stitches and then casting on for steeks, which are cut open later and stitched down.

How to make a 3-st, one-row buttonhole

With the yarn at the front of your work, slip the next stitch purlwise, then take the yarn to the back of the work between your needles.

*Slip 1 stitch purlwise. Pass the first slipped stitch over the new slipped stitch and off the right needle; repeat from * once more. Pass the remaining slipped stitch purlwise back to the left needle and turn, so that the wrong side of the work is facing you.

Now, using the cable method, cast on 2 stitches. Then cast on 1 more stitch but leave it on the right needle, bring the yarn to the front of the work and slip this final cast-on stitch onto the left needle and turn, so that the right side of the work is facing you.

Slip the next stitch knitwise, and slip the last cast-on st over it and off the right needle. Your buttonhole is complete!

INSTRUCTIONS

With MC and smaller circular needles, make a slip knot and place on needle as the first st, leaving a long tail for casting on. Cast on 1 st using the long-tail cast-on method, then cast on 2 sts using the twisted German cast-on method. *Cast on 2 sts using the long-tail cast-on method, cast on 2 sts using the twisted German cast-on method; repeat from * until there are 288 (288: 336: 336: 384) sts on the needle.

Join to work in the round, being careful not to twist. Place marker for beginning of round.

Follow written pattern below and refer to chart for colourwork placement only.

Hem

Rib Round: *K2, p2; repeat from * to end of round.

Work Rib Round another 13 (11: 13: 11: 12) times.

Body

Change to larger circular needles.

Work colourwork section, repeating the 24-stitch pattern 12 (12: 14: 14: 16) times per round, and placing markers every 24 sts to denote repeats, if desired, on first of these rounds.

Continue in colourwork pattern until you have completed Round 120 (108: 120: 95: 113), ending last round 10 sts before end of round.

Shape armholes and set steeks

Next Round: Cast off 11 sts, pattern until you have 133 (133: 157: 157: 181) sts on your needles, cast off the next 11 sts, pattern 133 (133: 157: 157: 181) sts to end of round,

noting that the first of these sts will already be on your right needle after casting off. DO NOT BREAK YARN.

You will now cast on for steeks across both armholes.

Next Round: Using the backwards loop method and MC, cast on 7 sts across left underarm cast-off, pattern across 133 (133: 157: 157: 181) sts for Front, cast on 7 sts across right underarm cast-off, pattern across 133 (133: 157: 157: 181) sts for Back. 280 (280: 328: 328: 376) sts total; 133 (133: 157: 157: 181) sts each for Front and Back and 7 sts per steek.

When working steek stitches, use two colours, alternating every other stitch to create a chequerboard or stripe effect.

Steeks should always be worked as follows: P1, k5, p1.

Purling at the edges of the steek allows you to fold back the edge easily later.

Continue working straight, keeping Front and Back pattern and steek correct, until you have completed Round 159 (146: 178: 146: 178).

Shape front neck

You will now shape the front neck. To do this, you will need to work back and forth in rows, turning at neck edge each time. While shaping front neck, continue working steeks across armholes, purling in pattern on WS rows and stranding yarn not in use across WS of work.

Next Round: Work steek, then pattern across next 45 (46: 54: 56: 66) sts for Left Front, pattern across next 43 (41: 49: 45: 49) sts for Front neck and leave on a holder or waste yarn, pattern until you have 45 (46: 54: 56: 66) sts for Right Front on right needle after putting sts on holder, work steek, pattern across 133 (133: 157: 157: 181) sts for Back. 237 (239: 279: 283: 327) sts total; 45 (46: 54: 56: 66) sts each for Left and Right Fronts, 133 (133: 157: 157: 181) sts for Back and 7 sts per steek.

Break yarn.

With WS facing, rejoin yarn to neck edge of Left Front.

Next row (WS): Maintaining pattern and steeks, work to end.

Pattern continues overleaf

Dec Row (RS): K1, ssk, patt to last 3 sts, k2tog, k1. 2 sts dec'd.

Work 1 row straight.

Rep Dec Row. 2 sts dec'd.

Rep last 2 rows another 2 times. 229 (231: 271: 275: 319) sts total; 41 (42: 50: 52: 62) sts each for Left and Right Fronts, 133 (133: 157: 157: 181) sts for Back and 7 sts per steek.

Work 7 (13: 13: 13: 13) rows straight, ending after a WS row.

You will now cast off steeks and work Back and Fronts separately.

Next Row (RS): Pattern 41 (42: 50: 52: 62) Right Front sts to steek, cast off next 7 steek sts, pattern until you have the 133 (133: 157: 157: 181) sts for Back on your right needle, cast off next 7 steek sts, pattern 41 (42: 50: 52: 62) Left Front sts to end, noting that the first of these sts will already be on your right needle after casting off.

Shape left front shoulder

Turn and continue on these last 41 (42: 50: 52: 62) Left Front sts only.

Starting with a WS row, work straight in pattern for 9 (5: 5: 5: 5) more rows, ending after a WS row.

Next Row (RS buttonhole): Pattern 8 (9: 17: 19: 29) sts, work a buttonhole (see pattern note), [pattern 9 sts, work a buttonhole] twice, pattern 6 sts to end.

Work straight in pattern for 8 (6: 6: 6: 6) rows, ending after a RS row.

Create left front shoulder flap

Change to MC only and smaller needles.

Next Row (WS): Patt to last 4 (5: 13: 15: 25) sts and turn, leaving these 4 (5: 13: 15: 25) sts on waste yarn. 37 sts.

Work in st st for 8 (6: 6: 6: 6) rows, ending after a WS row.

Next row (RS): Purl to create a turning ridge.

Beginning with a purl (WS) row, work in st st for 8 (6: 6: 6: 6) rows, ending after a WS row.

Next Row (RS buttonhole): K4, work a buttonhole (see pattern note), [k9, work a buttonhole] twice, k6 to end.

Work in st st for 9 (5: 5: 5: 5) more rows, ending after a WS row.

Leave on a stitch holder or waste yarn. Break yarn.

Shape right front shoulder

Rejoin yarn with RS facing to 41 (42: 50: 52: 62) Right Front sts.

Work straight in pattern for 18 (12: 12: 12: 12) rows, ending after a WS row.

Leave on a stitch holder or waste yarn. Break yarn.

Shape back neck

Rejoin yarn with RS facing to 133 (133: 157: 157: 181) Back sts and pattern across 51 (49: 57: 53: 57) sts for Right Back and leave on a stitch holder or waste yarn, pattern across next 52 (50: 58: 54: 58) sts for back neck and leave on a second stitch holder or separate piece of waste yarn, pattern across Left Back to last 4 (5: 13: 15: 25) sts and turn, leaving these 4 (5: 13: 15: 25) sts on waste yarn. 37 sts.

Create left back shoulder flap

Change to MC only and smaller needles.

Work in st st for 8 (6: 6: 6: 6) rows, ending after a RS row.

Next Row (WS): Knit to create a turning ridge.

Work in st st for 18 (12: 12: 12: 12) more rows, ending after a WS row.

Leave on a stitch holder or waste yarn.

Interim finishing

Right shoulder

With RS facing each other and working from the armhole edge inwards, rejoin MC. Using Kitchener stitch, graft the 41 (42: 50: 52: 62) Right Front sts together with the 41 (42: 50: 52: 62) Right Back sts.

Pattern continues overleaf

Natural colourway

- ☐ Knit
- ☐ Pattern repeat
- ■ 101 Natural Black
- ☐ 104 Natural White

COLOUR CODE	NO. 25G BALLS NEEDED				
	XS	S	M	L	XL
101 >	9	11	11	12	14
104 >	8	9	10	11	12

Neck chart

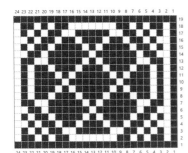

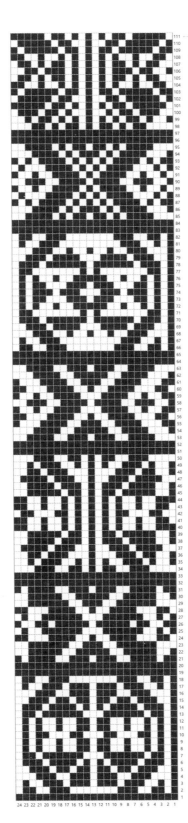

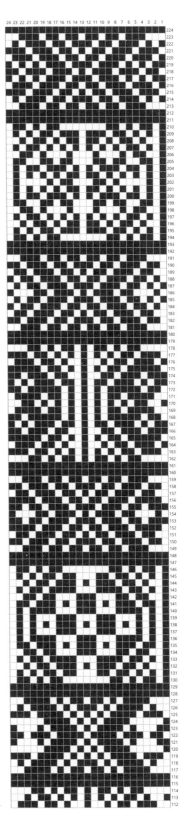

Left shoulder

Fold the Left Back shoulder sts worked in MC only in half at WS knit row (with WS together), and catch down the long edge to form the Left Back shoulder flap.

Fold the Left Front shoulder sts at the MC WS knit row (with WS together) and catch down the long edge to form the Left Front shoulder flap, ensuring that you line up buttonholes on MC section with buttonholes on colourwork section.

Using needle and thread, oversew edges of each of the three buttonholes on MC and colourwork sections so that they each form a single buttonhole between both layers of fabric.

With WS facing each other and working from the armhole edge inwards, rejoin MC. Using Kitchener stitch, graft together the first 4 (5: 13: 15: 25) sts of Left Back shoulder with first 4 (5: 13: 15: 25) sts of Left Front shoulder.

Lay garment flat so that the shoulder seams are sitting at back, and place a waste yarn marker at the left and right armhole edges of the new natural fold at the top of the shoulder.

Sleeves

With MC and smaller DPNs or short circular needles, cast on 61 (59: 69: 67: 73) sts.

Join to work in the round, being careful not to twist. Place marker for beginning of round.

Knit 2 rounds.

This edging is worked by using two separate strands of the same colour, alternating them across each round. In this way, you create a single-colour form of stranded colourwork, which will remain at the same tension as the colourwork section you have already worked.

For the second strand, pull from the centre of the ball.

If you are following the chart, you will see a symbol indicating when to use the second strand, given here as kwss.

Round 1: *K1, kwss; repeat from * to last st, k1.

Round 2: *Kwss, k1; repeat from * to last st, kwss.

Repeat last 2 rounds once more.

Change to larger DPNs or short circular needles.

Beginning with st 19 (20: 15: 16: 25) of chart and row 1 and ending with st 7 (6: 11: 10: 1), continue in colourwork pattern, working 17 (15: 17: 17: 19) rows of chart as set, noting that you will need to work partial repeats of the pattern at beginning and end of rounds.

Shape sleeve

Taking new sts into colourwork pattern, shape sleeves as follows.

Inc Round: K1, M1R, k to last st, M1L, k1. 2 sts inc'd.

Work 3 (1: 1: 1: 1) rounds straight.

Repeat Inc Round once more. 2 sts inc'd.

Repeat last 4 (2: 2: 2: 2) rounds another 30 (4: 22: 21: 29) times. 125 (71: 117: 113: 135) sts.

Sizes S, M, L and XL only

Work 3 (3: 3: 3) rounds straight.

Repeat Inc Round once more. 2 sts inc'd.

Repeat last 4 (4: 4: 4) rounds another 28 (22: 19: 18) times. 125 (129: 163: 153: 173) sts.

All sizes

Work another 5 (5: 4: 5: 4) rounds straight, ending last round 5 sts before end of round.

Cast off next 10 sts. 115 (119: 153: 143: 163) sts.

Leave sts on a holder.

Repeat pattern for second sleeve.

Pattern continues overleaf

Traditional colourway

Legend:
- ☐ Knit
- ☐ Pattern repeat
- ■ 101 Natural Black
- ☐ 289 Gold
- ■ 587 Madder
- ■ 726 Prussian
- ☐ 104 Natural White

COLOUR CODE	NO. 25G BALLS NEEDED				
	XS	S	M	L	XL
101 >	5	6	6	7	7
289 >	6	6	7	7	8
587 >	4	4	5	5	5
726 >	4	4	5	5	5
104 >	4	5	5	6	6

Neck chart

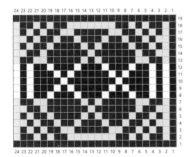

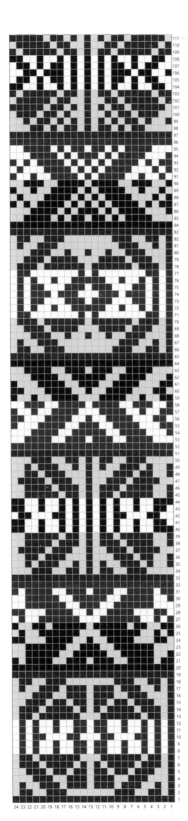

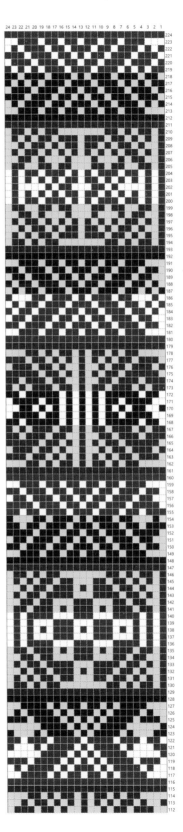

Finishing

Neck edging

With RS facing, using MC and smaller DPNs or short circular needles, and beginning at side edge of left shoulder opening, pick up and knit 16 (11: 11: 11: 11) sts across left front shoulder flap, pick up and knit 36 (33: 37: 33: 35) sts down first side of front neck, knit across 43 (41: 49: 45: 49) held sts for front neck, pick up and knit 36 (33: 37: 33: 35) sts up second side of front neck, pattern across 51 (49: 57: 53: 57) held sts for back neck and 17 (13: 13: 13: 13) sts across MC back shoulder flap. DO NOT JOIN. 199 (180: 204: 188: 200) sts.

You will now adjust your stitch count to give 192 (168: 192: 168: 192) sts from left front shoulder flap to beg of MC back shoulder flap, plus 17 (13: 13: 13: 13) sts across MC back shoulder flap for a total of 209 (181: 205: 181: 205) sts.

Follow instructions for your size as follows:

Size XS (WS inc): P17 for back shoulder flap, p2 (M1P, p18) 10 times. 209 sts; 17 sts for back shoulder flap and 192 sts around neck edge.

Size S (WS inc): P13 for back shoulder flap, M1P, purl to end. 181 sts; 13 sts for back shoulder flap and 168 sts around neck edge.

Size M (WS inc): P13 for back shoulder flap, M1P, purl to end. 205 sts; 13 sts for back shoulder flap and 192 sts around neck edge.

Size L (WS dec): P13 for back shoulder flap, (p2tog, p23) 7 times. 181 sts; 13 sts for back shoulder flap and 168 sts around neck edge.

Size XL (WS inc): P13 for back shoulder flap, p2 (M1P, p37) 5 times. 205 sts; 13 sts for back shoulder flap and 192 sts around neck edge.

All sizes

209 (181: 205: 181: 205) sts. Beginning with a RS row, work Row 1 of Neck chart, repeating 24-stitch pattern 8 (7: 8: 7: 8) times per row, and then working another 17 (13: 13: 13: 13) sts in pattern across left back shoulder flap.

Work 2 more rows as set, keeping pattern correct and ending after a RS row.

Next Row (WS buttonhole): Pattern to last 11 (7: 7: 7: 7) sts, work a buttonhole, pattern to end.

Work rows 5–13 of Neck chart, ending after a RS row.

Work a WS buttonhole row once more.

Work Rows 15–18 of Neck chart, ending after a WS row.

Break off other yarns and continue in MC only.

Next Row (RS): Knit to last 3 sts, k2tog, k1. 208 (180: 204: 180: 204) sts.

Rib Row: *P2, k2; repeat from * to end of row.

Work Rib Row another 3 times.

Cast off in rib.

Finishing

Crochet 2 chains up each steek, 1 st either side of the central stitch.

Carefully cut open each steek with a pair of small sharp scissors, by cutting through the central stitch. Fold back, using the purl stitch as a guide, and catch down the edges to the inside of the garment.

Place a waste yarn marker in waste yarn at centre of shoulder.

With a smaller circular needle, pick up but do not knit 57 (59: 76: 71: 81) sts up first side of armhole, pick up but do not knit 1 st at centre of shoulder in line with waste yarn marker, pick up but do not knit 57 (59: 76: 71: 81) sts down second side of armhole. 115 (119: 153: 143: 163) sts.

Line up centre of top sleeve with waste yarn marker.

Using Kitchener stitch, graft sleeve into armhole, leaving underarm and sleeve top cast-offs ungrafted.

Join underarm and sleeve top cast offs together using false grafting.

Sew on buttons.

Weave in ends and block to measurements given at the beginning of the pattern.

Striped
colourway

☐	Knit
☐	Pattern repeat
▨	825 Olive
■	101 Natural Black
▨	102 Shaela
▨	106 Mooskit
☐	104 Natural White
▨	578 Rust

	NO. 25G BALLS NEEDED				
COLOUR CODE	XS	S	M	L	XL
825 >	5	6	6	7	7
101 >	5	6	6	7	7
102 >	3	4	4	4	4
106 >	4	4	5	5	5
104 >	4	4	5	5	5
578 >	3	4	4	4	4

Neck chart

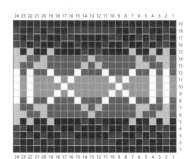

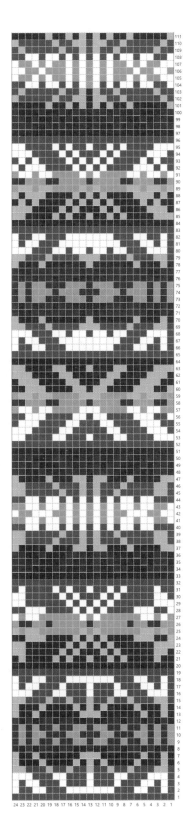

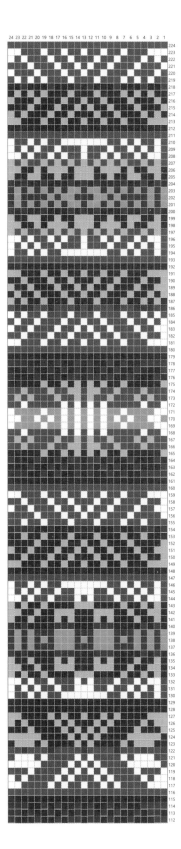

HORIZONTAL SCARF

By using different colour combinations, this pattern takes advantage of the versatility of Fair Isle motifs. This scarf design explores not only colourwork but also structure. The scarf is knitted horizontally and worked in individual panels that are sewn together. Each panel explores colour, using the same arrangement of the Muckle Flooers and Fivey Flooers motifs.

SIZE	AFTER SEAMING	PER SECTION
Finished circumference	214cm 84¼in	72cm 28¼in
Finished height	34cm 13½in	34cm 13½in

YARN

Jamieson's of Shetland,
Shetland Spindrift 4ply weight,
100% Shetland wool,
105m (115yd) per 25g ball

Natural colourway

- **15** × 101 Natural Black **MC**
- **12** × 104 Natural White

Traditional colourway

- **7** × 101 Natural Black **MC**
- **7** × 289 Gold
- **6** × 587 Madder
- **6** × 726 Prussian
- **7** × 104 Natural White

Striped colourway

- **6** × 825 Olive
- **7** × 101 Natural Black
- **6** × 102 Shaela
- **5** × 106 Mooskit
- **5** × 104 Natural White
- **5** × 578 Rust

Opposite: Bonfire at North Haven
Scarf knitted by Nancy Hunter
Below: Scarf knitted by Nancy Hunter

TENSION

27 stitches and 30 rows (rounds) to 10cm (4in), measured over blocked stranded colourwork, using 3.25mm (US 3, UK 10) needles.

If necessary, change your needle size to achieve the stated tension.

NEEDLES & NOTIONS

3.25mm (US 3, UK 10) circular needle, 40cm (16in) long

Tapestry needle

1 stitch marker plus 7 stitch markers, in a contrasting colour (optional)

Crochet hook in similar size to needle, or smaller if working steek (see Option B)

Small crochet hook if working steek (see Option B)

Needle and polyester or wool thread if working steek (see Option B)

Small sharp scissors if working steek (see Option B)

NOTE

When working colourwork sections, strand colour not in use evenly across the back (wrong side) of your work.

All chart rows should be read from right to left when working in the round.

When working flat, read RS rows from right to left and WS rows from left to right.

This scarf is made up of three separate colourwork sections and there are two ways you can make it.

Option A

Work each section flat and then stitch the sections together along short edges.

Option B

Work each section as a tube with a steek, cut it open and then stitch the sections together along short edges.

Which option should you choose?

Option A will give a slightly neater finish, but has the disadvantage of working stranded colourwork from the wrong side on alternate rows, which makes it harder to see what you're doing.

Option B requires you to work a steek, which is a more advanced technique, but means that you can work the stranded colourwork in rounds, with the right side facing you at all times. However, the steek will create a less refined edge at the seams and be visible on the wrong side of the fabric.

We have given instructions here for both options. The scarf in the photographs was made using Option A.

There is a different Main Colour (MC) for each section for the Traditional and Striped colourways, so refer to your charts for which yarn to treat as the MC in each section.

INSTRUCTIONS: Option A

Note that there is a balancing stitch at the beginning of section 1 and the end of section 3 outside of the main pattern repeats.

Each of the three sections can be worked entirely from the charts, repeating the 24-stitch pattern 8 times per row and placing markers every 24 sts to denote repeats if desired on Row 10.

If this is your preferred method, follow chart until you have completed Row 102. Read sections below on Lower and Upper edging before working Rows 1–9 and 94–102.

When Row 102 is complete, cast off knitwise.

Alternatively, follow written pattern overleaf and refer to chart for colourwork section only.

Pattern continues overleaf

Natural
colourway

☐ Knit
◇ Kwss
▯ Repeat pattern

■ 101 Natural Black
☐ 104 Natural White

HORIZONTAL SCARF

Section 1

Lower edging

With MC, cast on 194 sts, using the long-tail cast-on method.

Beginning with a WS (purl) row, work 3 rows in st st.

The next 6 rows of edging are worked by using 2 separate strands of the same colour, alternating them across each row, with the strand not in use held at the WS of the work. In this way, you create a single-colour form of stranded colourwork, which will prevent the top edge of the scarf from rolling over while remaining at the same tension as the colourwork section you will work next.

For the second strand, pull from the centre of the ball.

If you are following the chart, you will see a symbol indicating when to use the second strand, given here as kwss and pwss.

Row 4 (RS): *K1, kwss; rep from * to end of row.

Row 5 (WS): *P1, pwss; rep from * to end of row.

Repeat last 2 rows twice more.

Main section

Work colourwork section, following Rows 10–93 of Section 1 chart, repeating the 24-stitch pattern 8 times per row and placing markers every 24 sts to denote repeats, if desired, on first of these rounds.

Upper edging

Row 94 (RS): *K1, kwss; rep from * to end of row.

Row 95 (WS): *P1, pwss; rep from * to end of row.

Rep last 2 rows twice more.

Beginning with an RS row, work 3 rows in st st.

Cast off knitwise.

Finishing

Weave in ends and block to measurements given at the beginning of the pattern.

Repeat for Sections 2 and 3.

Seam pieces together along short edges using mattress stitch.

INSTRUCTIONS: Option B

Note that there is a balancing stitch at the beginning of Section 1 and the end of Section 3 outside of the main pattern repeats.

Each of the three sections can be worked entirely from the charts, repeating the 24-stitch pattern 8 times per round and placing markers every 24 sts to denote repeats, if desired, on Round 10.

Work the Lower Edging in rows and then cast on for the steek on Row 10 and join to work in the round, casting off for the steek after Round 93 and working the Upper Edging in rows until you have completed Row 102. Read section overleaf on Lower and Upper edging before working Rows 1–9 and 94–102.

When Row 102 is complete, cast off knitwise from the WS.

Alternatively, follow written pattern overleaf and refer to chart for colourwork section only.

Pattern continues overleaf

Taditional colourway

	Knit
◇	Kwss
	Repeat pattern
■	101 Natural Black

	289 Gold
	587 Madder
	726 Prussian
	104 Nautral White

⬥ 133 ⬥

HORIZONTAL SCARF

Lower edging

With MC, cast on 194 sts, using the long-tail cast-on method.

Beginning with a WS (purl) row, work 3 rows in st st.

The next 6 rows of edging are worked by using two separate strands of the same colour, alternating them across each row, with the strand not in use held at the WS of the work. In this way, you create a single-colour form of stranded colourwork, which will prevent the top edge of the scarf from rolling over while remaining at the same tension as the colourwork section you will work next.

For the second strand, pull from the centre of the ball.

If you are following the chart, you will see a symbol indicating when to use the second strand, given here as kwss and pwss.

Row 4 (RS): *K1, kwss; rep from * to end of row.

Row 5 (WS): *P1, pwss; rep from * to end of row.

Repeat last 2 rows twice more.

Main section

Round 10: Using the backwards loop method and MC, cast on 7 sts, work colourwork section, repeating the 24-stitch pattern 8 times and placing markers every 24 sts to denote repeats if desired. Do not turn. Join to work in the round, being careful not to twist. Place marker for beginning of round. 201 sts; 194 sts for Main section and 7 sts for steek.

When working steek across remaining rounds, use two colours, alternating every other stitch to create a chequerboard or stripe effect on the steek stitches.

Steeks should always be worked as follows: P1, k5, p1.

Purling at the edges of the steek allows you to fold back the edge easily later.

Work colourwork section, following Rounds 11–93 of Section 1 chart.

Upper edging

You will now work in rows again.

Row 94 (RS): Cast off 7 steek sts, *K1, kwss; rep from * to end of row, noting that the first of these sts will already be on your right needle after casting off. 194 sts.

Row 95 (WS): *P1, pwss; rep from * to end of row.

Repeat last 2 rows twice more.

Beginning with a RS row, work 3 rows in st st.

Cast off knitwise.

Finishing

Weave in ends and block to measurements given at the beginning of the pattern.

Repeat for Sections 2 and 3.

Crochet two chains up each steek, 1 st either side of the central stitch.

Carefully cut open each steek with a pair of small sharp scissors, by cutting through the central stitch. Fold back, using the purl stitch as a guide, and catch down the edges to the WS of the fabric.

Seam pieces together along short edges using mattress stitch.

134

Striped
Colourway

☐ Knit	■ 825 Olive	▦ 106 Mooskit
◇ Kwss	■ 101 Natural Black	☐ 104 Natural White
▯ Repeat pattern	■ 102 Shaela	■ 578 Rust

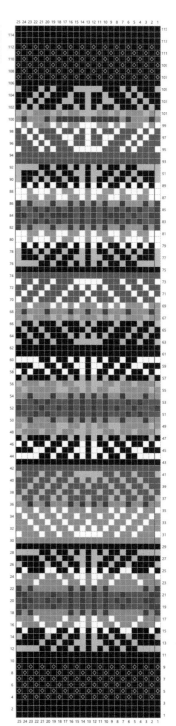

135

TECHNIQUES

'Makking' with wires.

Long-tail cast on (thumb method)

To figure out where to tie your slip knot, first measure out a length of yarn 3¹/₂ times the width of what you plan to make. So for a 15cm (6in) wide scarf, measure out approximately 53cm (21in) of yarn, and at that point, make a loop.

Bring the yarn that is on top around to the back of the loop.

Slide the knitting needle under the yarn that is behind the loop.

Pull both lengths of yarn so that the slip knot is just grazing the needle. Try to resist the temptation to tug on the yarn, making your stitches too snug around the needle. If your cast on is too tight, your first row of knitting will be quite unpleasant and your finished piece will have a taut edge, so be gentle.

Loop the end of the yarn (the 'tail') around your thumb. The tail should come from the needle, around the back of your thumb to the front of your thumb.

With the tip of the needle, pick up the front strand of the loop in an away-from-you motion (i.e. from front to back), sliding the needle up your thumb.

With your right hand, bring the yarn that is coming from the ball (the 'working yarn') behind and around the needle in an anti-clockwise direction.

Now, with a toward-you motion (i.e. from back to front), bring the needle through the loop on your thumb, allowing the loop to pass over the tip of the needle.

Slip your thumb out of the loop and pull both strands of yarn to gently secure the stitch on the needle.

Position a new loop on your thumb and continue to cast on in this manner until you have the correct number of stitches.

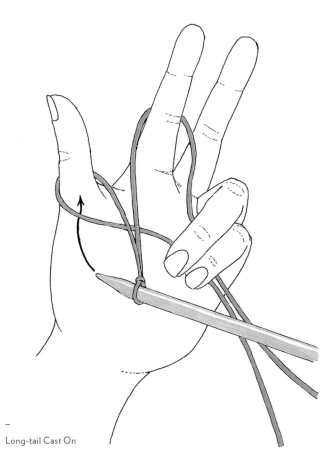

Long-tail Cast On

Long-tail cast on (sling method)

As per the previous method, measure out a length of yarn 3½ times the width of what you plan to make, and at that point, make a slip knot.

Bring the yarn that is on top around to the back of the loop.

Slide the knitting needle under the yarn that is behind the loop.

Pull both lengths of yarn so that the slip knot is just grazing the needle. Be gentle when pulling so as not to make the yarn taut.

With the long tail in front and the working yarn behind, you are ready to set up the sling shot. Put the index and thumb finger of your left hand together and in between the two strands of yarn, then open your fingers so that the needle and slip knot sit in the middle, between your index finger and thumb. With the remaining three fingers of your left hand, grab the tails and gently pull the needle back holding the first stitch (the slip knot) with the index finger of your right hand. Your sling cast on is set.

Take the needle towards your left thumb and pass it under the yarn wrapped around your thumb, then take the needle towards your left index and pass it over the yarn wrapped around your index and pull the yarn through to create the new stitch. Repeat until you have the desired number of stitches.

Twisted German cast on

The twisted German cast on creates a flexible edge. To start, work as per the long-tail cast on sling method and set your sling.

Take the needle towards your left thumb and pass it under the two yarns wrapped around your thumb and back on itself down your thumb, through the middle of the two strands of yarn wrapped around the thumb. Take the needle towards your left index finger and pass it over the yarn wrapped around your index finger and pull the yarn through the centre of the twist or lower part of the 'X' formed by the twisted yarn to make your stitch. Repeat until you have the desired number of stitches.

Backwards loop cast on

The backwards loop cast on is a great way of casting on in the middle of work using one strand of yarn.

Grab your working yarn with the fingers of your left hand, leaving your thumb free. Take the yarn around the outside of your left thumb and put the needle through the yarn from the bottom of the thumb; slip the yarn off your thumb and your stitch is made. Repeat until you have the desired number of stitches.

Backwards Loop Cast On

Knit (K)

With your cast-on stitches on the left-hand needle, place the right-hand needle through the first stitch, entering the stitch from front to back (the needle points away from you). Wrap the yarn around the right-hand needle in an anti-clockwise direction and with the same needle pull the yarn through so that you create a new stitch, which is now on the right-hand needle. Slip the 'knitted' stitch off the left-hand needle. Repeat this process.

Purl (P)

Instead of the right-hand needle entering the stitches from front to back, the needle enters from back to front (the needle points towards you). Wrap the yarn around the right-hand needle in a clockwise direction, pushing the yarn through the stitch to create a new one, which is now on the right-hand needle. Slip the 'purled' stitch off the left-hand needle. Repeat this process.

Make one (M1)

Working into the place where the increase is to be made, insert your left needle from the back to the front, picking up the bar between the two stitches. Insert the right needle through the 'made' stitch from front to back and knit one stitch. This twists it to create the stitch. If working M1 on purl side, you purl the newly 'made' stitch.

Decrease (Dec)

When more than one stitch is suspended from a stitch, they can hang in different orientations. The first stitch could be on top of the second stitch (when seen from the right side) or the reverse, leaning to the left or the right. The order of stitches is important, both for appearance and for the way it pulls the fabric.

K2tog (knit two together)

Work to the two stitches to be decreased, insert the right-hand needle into the first two stitches as if to knit, wrap yarn around needle in normal manner, slip the two stitches off together and drop them. This creates a right-leaning decrease.

K2tog-L (knit two together – left)

A left-leaning decrease that is the mirror of K2tog and produces a neater finish than other left-leaning decreases such as SSK. The key to making this stitch work is to pull excess yarn from the second stitch before letting it drop off the needle.

Cast off

Knit 2 stitches. Take 1st stitch on right needle and pass it over the 2nd stitch. Knit one stitch and pass the 1st stitch over the 2nd stitch. Repeat this process until you have fully cast off. When the last stitch is on the right needle, take the tail of the yarn and pull it through the last stitch to secure. Weave the tail end into the reverse of the knitting and trim the end of the tail.

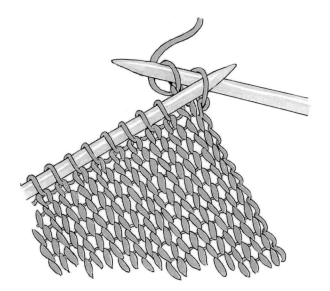

Casting Off

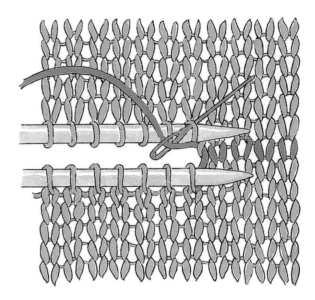

Kitchener Stitch

Kitchener stitch (graft)

This is a way of joining two pieces of knitting together. It essentially involves sewing a row of knitting in between two raw or live ends.

Lay both ends on a flat surface so that the knit side is facing up and the raw ends/ stitches are facing each other. Thread your tapestry needle with MC yarn.

Insert the tapestry needle purlwise into the first stitch on the lower piece, then knitwise into the first stitch on the upper piece. Pull the yarn through, ensuring you maintain the same tension as the rest of your knitting.

Insert the needle knitwise into the first stitch on the lower piece again, pull the yarn through and slide the stitch off the knitting needle. Insert the needle purlwise into the next stitch on the lower piece and pull the yarn through. Insert the needle purlwise into the first stitch on the upper piece, pull the yarn through and slide the stitch off the knitting needle. Insert the needle knitwise into the next stitch on the upper piece and pull the yarn through.

Repeat from * to * until you reach the end of the row.

Mattress stitch

This is a method of joining two sides together. It gives you an invisible finish between the two pieces. Unlike Kitchener stitch, you work the thread between each stitch, instead of through them. The thread is drawn underneath the 'bar', which is the stitch that runs behind the V-shaped stitch of the right side.

With the knit side of the pieces facing you, lay the sides to be joined next to each other, ensuring that the rows are lined up as accurately as possible. You will be working between these end courses of stitches to join them up. Seam the stitches, working one stitch in from the outside edge, from one side to the other.

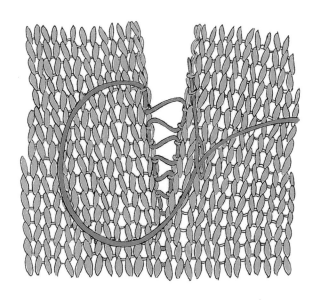

Mattress Stitch

Crochet for steeking

With a crochet hook and your work on the right side, take a strand of yarn and pull it through the back loop in between stitches, creating a loop. Keeping the new loop on the crochet hook, pick up the strand of your working yarn and pass it through creating a knot. Holding the working yarn behind your work, crochet a chain along the two lines of stitches by putting your hook through the back loop between the following stitches and pulling through the strand of working yarn. Continue until you have completed the length of work.

Steeking

A straight line is cut along the centre of a column of stitches, in order to make room for an opening or place to attach another piece. The steek itself is a bridge of extra stitches in which the cut is made, and is usually 6–10 stitches wide.

After the steek is cut, the edges are tucked down on the wrong side of the fabric in order to create a neat finish, or the adjacent stitches are sewn or crocheted together to prevent unravelling. The stitches can also be picked up and knit from. Alternatively, a sleeve can be made separately and sewn onto the steek. After the garment with a steek has been worn and washed a few times, the facings will felt and become durable finishes on the inside of the garment.

Blocking and pressing

Blocking involves pinning a piece of knitting onto a flat surface to ensure it has the correct shape and measurements. Taking the time to carefully block and press your garment will result in a better fitting and looking garment.

Traditionally, blocking is done by covering a piece of hardboard with a layer of wadding or foam and a piece of fabric, but you can purchase ready-made blocking panels. To block your piece, allow your garment to partially dry flat. When it is still moist but nearly dry, stretch the fabric to the desired shape and measurements and carefully pin it in place, making sure the edges are straight where necessary. Once your piece is pinned in place, allow it to dry completely, or you can press it. To press your knitting, place a tea towel or cloth on top of your work to protect the fabric. Steam iron your piece by pressing the iron down in sections without dragging it.

INDEX

143

ACKNOWLEDGEMENTS

Alicia Stephens

Alison Riley

Anette von Block

Anna Makila

Bobette Hardie Dorre

Connie Boster

Diana Sutton

Elbia Sylwestrzak

Gabi John

Heidi Sauser

Inca Cox

Iris Fitzgibbon

Isabel Sheets

Jackie Kirkham

Jana Hermann

Janneke Lewis

Judit Sogan

Julia Ryder

Lennice Lytle

Louise Bailey

Maj Corio

Margaret Milligan

Melanie Matt

Michael Austin

Nancy Hunter

Nicky Angeli

Noel Walker

Patricia Philbin

Paula Brown

Rebecca Snelling LeRoy

Samsara Chapman

Sara Levene

Sharon Bowden

Sheila Turcotte

Shuni Barrett

Sophie Bouchard-Skiffington

Sue Reeves

Suzanne Da Rosa

Val Smith

Vicky Sheppard

144

To Judith Hannam and her team at Kyle Books, I will be forever grateful for giving me such a great opportunity.
To Triona and Pat Thomson, and to Florrie Stout, thank you for teaching me the art of Fair Isle Knitting and allowing me to be part of the island's history.
To Dylan Thomas and Jeff Knowles, you are the most fabulous team I could have wish for. Here's to many years of amazing projects together.
To my kids, for loving me and supporting me even when I have not been there all the time because of work.
To all the amazing knitters above that made this project a reality, for their patience, all their feedback and their beautiful hands.

Closing endpaper: View of Kirki Geo and Sompal from Meoness